Jack Russell Terrier

2nd Edition

GET MORE!
Visit www.wiley.com/
go/jackrussellterrier

Catherine Romaine Brown

Howell
Book House™

Library of Congress Cataloging-in-Publication Data:
Brown, Catherine Romaine, (date).
Jack Russell terrier / Catherine Romaine Brown—2nd ed.
 p. cm.—(Your happy healthy pet)
ISBN-13: 978-0-471-74837-3 (cloth : alk. paper)
ISBN-10: 0-471-74837-4 (cloth : alk. paper)
1. Jack Russell terrier. I. Title. II. Series.
SF429.J27B76 2006
636.755—dc22
                                      2005034539

Printed in the United States of America

10 9 8 7 6 5 4 3

2nd Edition

Book design by Melissa Auciello-Brogan
Cover design by Michael J. Freeland
Illustrations in chapter 9 by Shelley Norris and Karl Brandt
Book production by Wiley Publishing, Inc. Composition Services

About the Author

Catherine Romaine Brown has been actively involved with Jack Russell Terriers for twenty-five years. She has served on the board of directors of the Jack Russell Terrier Club of America (JRTCA) and is currently the club's vice chair. Catherine is a conformation and field-working judge for the JRTCA and has been a state representative to the club for many years. She has judged many JRTCA-sanctioned terrier trials across the United States and the national trials of the Jack Russell Terrier Clubs of South Africa and Japan. She is also a member of the Dog Writers Association of America.

Catherine helped as the founder of Russell Rescue in the United States (now Russell Rescue Inc.) and is its president emeritus. She carried a Jack Russell in a pouch on horseback with a recognized pack of hounds until terrier work in the United States was banned by the Master of Foxhounds Association. Few Americans have had such an honor and opportunity.

She is also the author of *Jack Russell Terrier: Courageous Companion* in the Howell Book House Best of Breed Library. She holds a Master of Fine Arts degree and lives with her husband, Charles Streb III, in Livonia, New York, along with her small pack of terriers and her husband's Beagles.

About Howell Book House

Since 1961, Howell Book House has been America's premier publisher of pet books. We're dedicated to companion animals and the people who love them, and our books reflect that commitment. Our stable of authors—training experts, veterinarians, breeders, and other authorities—is second to none. And we've won more Maxwell Awards from the Dog Writers Association of America than any other publisher.

As we head toward the half-century mark, we're more committed than ever to providing new and innovative books, along with the classics our readers have grown to love. This year, we're launching several exciting new initiatives, including redesigning the Howell Book House logo and revamping our biggest pet series, Your Happy Healthy Pet™, with bold new covers and updated content. From bringing home a new puppy to competing in advanced equestrian events, Howell has the titles that keep animal lovers coming back again and again.

Contents

Shopping List

You'll need to do a bit of stocking-up before you bring your new dog or puppy home. Below is a basic list of some must-have supplies. For more detailed information on the selection of each item below, consult Chapter 5. For specific guidance on what grooming tools you'll need, review Chapter 7.

☐ Food dish   ☐ Crate

☐ Water dish   ☐ Nail clippers

☐ Dog food   ☐ Grooming tools

☐ Leash   ☐ Chew toys

☐ Collar   ☐ Toys

☐ ID tag

There are likely to be a few other items that you're dying to pick up before bringing your dog home. Use the following blanks to note any additional items you'll be shopping for.

☐ _____

☐ _____

☐ _____

☐ _____

☐ _____

☐ _____

☐ _____

☐ _____

☐ _____

☐ _____

☐ _____

☐ _____

Pet Sitter's Guide

We can be reached at (__)_____-_____ Cellphone (__)_____-_____

We will return on _____ (date) at _____ (approximate time)

Dog's Name _____

Breed, Age, and Sex _____

Important Names and Numbers

Vet's Name _____ Phone (__)_____- _____

Address_____

Emergency Vet's Name _____ Phone (__)_____- _____

Address_____

Poison Control _____ (or call vet first)

Other individual to contact in case of emergency _____

_____

Care Instructions

In the following three blanks let the sitter know what to feed, how much, and when; when the dog should go out; when to give treats; and when to exercise the dog.

Morning_____

_____

Afternoon_____

_____

Evening _____

_____

Medications needed (dosage and schedule) _____

_____

Any special medical conditions _____

_____

Grooming instructions _____

_____

My dog's favorite playtime activities, quirks, and other tips_____

_____

_____

Part I

The World of the Jack Russell Terrier

The Jack Russell Terrier

Muzzle

Stop

Occiput

Crest

Neck

Withers

Back

Loin

Croup

Scapula

Forearm

Wrist

Elbow

Dewclaw

Pastern

Stiffle
or Knee

Toes

Hock

Chapter 1

What Is a Jack Russell Terrier?

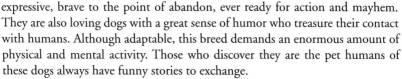

The Jack Russell Terrier is small in size but big in attitude. This dog is highly intelligent and expressive, brave to the point of abandon, ever ready for action and mayhem. They are also loving dogs with a great sense of humor who treasure their contact with humans. Although adaptable, this breed demands an enormous amount of physical and mental activity. Those who discover they are the pet humans of these dogs always have funny stories to exchange.

The Jack Russell comes in many sizes. They may be as small as ten inches at the top of the shoulder (called the withers) or as much as fifteen inches. The range in size ensures each dog will be the size needed for the work or the terrain he hunts in. JRTs come mostly white with brown or black markings. Whatever the size and shape, they have captured the hearts of all those charmed by their in-your-face attitude.

A Hunting Dog

The Jack Russell Terrier was developed to meet a formidable opponent below ground, the red fox (although JRTs also hunt other quarry). He was blended from now extinct strains of white-bodied terriers in Great Britain. With a dash of this working breed and a dash of that one, a hearty, healthy, keen, earth-working dog was shaped to the job of hunting.

The Latin word *terra* means earth, and that is the origin of the word "terrier"—earth dog. First and foremost, the Jack Russell Terrier is a hunting dog who works below ground. The dog's job is to keep the fox in check while the handler digs to both the fox and the dog. The dog has to possess a good voice to address the quarry below ground when located, to help keep the prey at bay, and to help the handler locate the dog by sound.

Everything about the dog reflects his job as hunter. It is said about the Jack Russell Terrier that where the fox can go, so must the terrier. This terrier's structure is modeled after that of the vixen (female fox). Like the fox, the Jack Russell must be well angulated and possess a small, compressible chest that enables him to maneuver in narrow earthen tunnels, often deeply below ground. The predominantly white coat is to help distinguish the dog from the fox when the hunter digs to where the dog holds his quarry at bay.

The intense character is all part of the hunting package, as well. Without a doubt, the Jack Russell is a courageous companion with the grit to hunt. The intelligence of the dog adds to the package, because the dog must independently solve problems below ground and hold himself back from taking on the quarry; a dog too eager to do battle below ground is apt to be lost.

The breed was not meant to harm the quarry he encounters. Still, JRTs do have different styles of work. Some are "hard" and engage their quarry with intent to inflict harm, while and some are "soft" and bay at or dislodge their quarry with their intense presence. All JRTs, however, should have the attitude, grit, and tenacity to confront larger and more formidable animals below ground. A very intelligent and cooperative Jack Russell may sometimes be called out of the den by the handler, but don't count on it!

The Jack Russell Terrier is first and foremost a hunting dog, developed to hunt quarry underground.

He's Not the Dog on TV

The Jack Russell Terrier is seen often on television and in the movies. Because they are expressive and exceptionally intelligent, they are often used in commercials, which gives the (incorrect) impression that this is a very mannerly dog. The dog you see in a commercial or on a television show is a very good actor and has a trainer who possesses a great deal of time and patience in teaching the dog a series of actions with hand signals or commands. The dog has spent a lot of time working—engaging his body and mind—to learn these moves. And when he is off camera, he is just as active as ever.

People get the idea all Jack Russells are like the television dogs, and then find the dog they have is locked in the "on" position, a rocket in motion. This is not the breed for the faint of heart or those who want a relaxed dog. The Jack Russell is ready for action and a lot of it!

The courage of the Jack Russell Terrier must be understood and accepted, whether you hunt with your dog or not. The dog's behavior may be described as total abandon. The instincts of the dog may make him act with single-mindedness in both work and play. You must be prepared to protect the dog from himself and always expect the unexpected.

Active, Determined Companions

Jack Russells relish close contact with the humans they love. They are very adaptable in many ways, but they do demand enormous amounts of physical and mental activity that are meaningful and satisfying to the dog. It is not easy to wear one out.

Jack Russells also have an assertive nature and require discipline and acceptance of their pluck and courage. They pack a big-dog attitude. They can sometimes be bullies to the biggest dogs they encounter, but they can also curl up for a nap next to a beloved companion.

There are many ways to provide fun outlets for the dog's energy. If you spend time tossing a ball or Frisbee at a set time each day, the dog will anticipate this quality activity time. It is wise not to encourage too much tug of war, because these dogs can develop an attitude of always wanting to be the winner, which may encourage behavior that is too assertive. Arrange the game of tug or toss so you and the dog take turns winning. The Jack Russell Terrier needs to know that the humans in his family, including the children, hold a rank in the family pack that is higher than his. This is not the dog to lend your car keys or credit cards to.

JRTs and Children

One of the most charming qualities of Jack Russells is their gentle and kindly nature toward children. The dog may be capable of being unusually friendly with small children provided the child understands how to handle the terrier.

JRTs do adore their children, but they will not tolerate teasing or abuse.

The intelligence of the dog and the strength of his presence mean he will not tolerate abuse from children. This is not a dog who takes well to punishment. He may defend himself if pushed too far, even from accidental abuse. Adult supervision is always suggested. JRTs fare better with children over 6 years of age. Some, however, adore their children and will allow themselves to be put in baby carriages and dressed in doll clothes.

Not a Latchkey Dog

This is a very adaptable dog who craves an interesting lifestyle. For example, a Jack Russell is a good candidate to go to work with you every day—if you are lucky enough to have a job that permits this. Many will be happy to sleep near you for most of the day. But you can't park this dog silently all day while you work someplace far away from your Jack Russell. If you must leave a dog alone for nine or more hours a day unattended, this may not be the dog for you.

Jack Russells need a job and thrive when they are given a routine and have something to do. They are worse than little children when they're bored. A bored dog may bark to fill his days—which may also fill your neighbors with annoyance. The protests can be very vocal; this is a dog bred to use his voice when hunting to work quarry.

You will need reliable containment if you leave your Jack Russell for even half a second. They can escape most containment that is not a maximum-security setup. Your Jack Russell can dig under fences that lack proper turned-under safe wire buried under the edges of a pen or dog run. They can climb human style up and over chain-link fences. They can jump four feet up effort-lessly from a standstill.

It is unthinkable to keep any dog tied out on a rope, chain, or cable, especially the active Jack Russell. It is also cruel to leave such an active dog in a crate for long hours. This active dog does not fare well with such treatment. Expect this dog to require a great deal more of your time and attention than you ever imagined.

Learn about and meet the breed before selecting a Jack Russell Terrier. Be prepared for the dog and what he will need. Many people can make adjustments and work out what both they and the dog require to be happy. The need to surrender a dog can be prevented with some adjustments by both dog and owner. But I cannot stress too strongly that this is not the dog for everyone.

The Jack Russell Terrier Standard

As stated by the Jack Russell Terrier Club of America (JRTCA), the largest breed club devoted to this breed, "Jack Russell Terriers are a type, or strain, of working terrier. They are not considered purebred in the sense that they have a broad genetic make-up, a broad standard, and do not breed true to type. This is a result of having been bred strictly for hunting since their beginning in the early 1800's, and their preservation as a working terrier since. The broad standard, varied genetic background based on years of restricted inbreeding and wide out-crossing, and great variety of size and type are the major characteristics that make this strain of terrier known as a Jack Russell such a unique, versatile working terrier."

Still, there are physical characteristics every Jack Russell should have

> The Jack Russell Terrier Club of America has more than 6,500 members and more than 18,000 dogs in its registry.

What Is a Breed Standard?

A breed standard is a detailed description of the perfect dog of that breed. Breeders use the standard as a guide in their breeding programs, and judges use it to evaluate the dogs in conformation classes. The standard for the Jack Russell Terrier is written by the national breed club, The Jack Russell Terrier Club of America, using guidelines established by the registry. You can read the entire Jack Russell Terrier standard at www.terrier.com.

The Parson Russell Terrier is a variant of the Jack Russell Terrier. It has a standard recognized by the AKC and the UKC. (See chapter 2 for how this variation came about.) You can read the AKC breed standard for the Parson Russell Terrier at www.akc.org.

in common, and these are described in the breed standard. The Jack Russell must be compact and in totally balanced proportions. The shoulders should be clean, the legs straight, and the chest easily spanned by average-sized hands at the widest part of the dog behind the shoulders. The chest must be compressible. This required conformation allows the terrier success below ground, where he must be able to maneuver underground in narrow dark tunnels to get to the very flexible fox.

In the following section, the words in quotes are taken from the breed standard written by the JRTCA. It begins by saying the Jack Russell "should impress with its fearless and happy disposition." The Jack Russell Terrier is "a sturdy, tough dog, very much on its toes all the time. . . . The body length must be in proportion to the height, and it should present a compact, balanced image, always being solid and in hard condition."

The dog should not be slack of muscle or overweight. Nothing should be exaggerated about the dog's appearance. A dog with a long back and stubby, crooked little legs is not acceptable. The dog should be a nice-looking, harmonious package, with everything in proportion.

He should move effortlessly, with both pull from the front end and drive from the back end. The topline of the dog (that is, the line of the back) should move smoothly when viewed from the side. The legs should be straight, without turned-in hocks or turned-out front feet.

The Jack Russell's head "should be well balanced and in proportion to the body. The skull should be flat, of moderate width at the ears, narrowing to the eyes." There should be a defined but not overly pronounced stop—the area where the muzzle meets the skull. "The length of the muzzle from the nose to the stop should be slightly shorter than the distance from the stop to the occiput," which is the back of the skull. "The nose should be black. The jaw should be powerful and well boned with strongly muscled cheeks."

The dog's eyes should be almond-shaped, dark, and "full of life and intelligence." The ears are "small, V-shaped drop ears carried forward close to the head." The ears should not stand up straight nor be thick and large like hound's ears.

The mouth of the Jack Russell Terrier has strong teeth and a scissors bite, which means the top teeth overlap the lower ones. A level bite, where the upper and lower teeth meet, is also acceptable. The neck of the Jack Russell is "clean and muscular, of good length, gradually widening at the shoulders." The good neck allows the dog to spar with quarry below ground and adds to his athleticism while at work.

"The chest of the Jack Russell Terrier should be shallow and narrow and the front legs not set too widely apart, giving an athletic rather than heavily chested appearance." The chest needs to be flexible and compressible to enhance the dog's ability to work up close to the quarry in bending and winding narrow tunnels below ground. A large-chested dog is limited in hunting below ground because he cannot fit in a narrow earthen den.

"The back should be strong, straight and, in proportion to the height of the terrier, giving a balanced image. The loin should be slightly arched." In other words, the entire structure of the dog is designed for strength, to able to hold up under hard work and move efficiently.

The feet of the Jack Russell Terrier need to be "round, hard padded, of cat-like appearance, neither turning in or out." The dog needs strong feet for digging and crossing varied terrain.

Effortless movement and great athleticism are hallmarks of the breed.

A JRT's coat provides protection against thorns and burrs as well as dampness.

The tail "should be set rather high, carried gaily and in proportion to body length, usually about four inches long, providing a good hand-hold." The tail is cropped at about three days old so it does not break while backing out of earth, and the dewclaws are removed. The tail is sometimes used as a handle of sorts to extricate the dog from the earth. It usually requires holding the dog's tail and hind legs to dislodge him from work below ground.

The coat is "smooth, without being so sparse as not to provide a certain amount of protection from the elements and undergrowth." The coat is so very important as the dog's protection. Sometimes JRTs are in the damp ground working long hours. The coat makes an enormous difference to the protection of the dog at work. The coat seems to resist thorns and burrs, and the dog can easily shake out loose dirt. The Jack Russell Terrier may wear a rough or a smooth coat, or it could be a combination of both, known as a broken coat. A broken-coated dog may have some tail or face furnishings (longer hairs).

As for color, the dog must be more than 51 percent white, with solid tan, black, or brown markings. White is handy to see when working in dirt with a dog who is face to face with a critter who is earth-colored. Brindle markings, made up of several different colors of hair, are not allowed because they indicate the blood of another breed.

Chapter 2

The Jack Russell's History

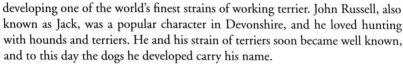

The Reverend John Russell lived between 1795 and 1883 in Devonshire, England. He contributed to developing one of the world's finest strains of working terrier. John Russell, also known as Jack, was a popular character in Devonshire, and he loved hunting with hounds and terriers. He and his strain of terriers soon became well known, and to this day the dogs he developed carry his name.

The Fox Terrier

The original strains of Fox Terriers were based on what were called White Terriers, which now are extinct. Many hunt kennels in Great Britain kept their own strains of terriers to work with their hounds. The hounds would give the fox chase, and the mounted staff and hunters would follow to observe and hear the hounds sing. Of course, chasing foxes with a pack of hounds and many riders is hardly an efficient method of fox control. It is more a country tradition and an active outing—part of the rich history of humans and hunting.

The hounds were always the aristocrats, and the terriers were the hunting partners of the hounds. Pedigrees were carefully kept on hounds, but many terriers were simply the product of one good working dog bred to another for the job of dislodging a fox the hounds had chased to ground.

When the fox was chased into an earthen den, the hounds and field of riders were moved back by the Master of Foxhounds so the terrier could enter the deep

Vicar of Swymbridge 1832/1880

Rev: John Russell

The Reverend John "Jack" Russell was a flamboyant man who adored his hounds and hunting.

underground passage. Sometimes a staff member would carry a terrier in a pouch on horseback so the terrier would be handy the minute she was needed to enter the earth for the foxhunters. The terrier willingly entered, and her intrusive presence below ground would give the fox the idea to move on and the chase could continue. The dog was not bred to do the fox harm.

The fox is a formidable opponent, larger and more at home in the earth. The Fox Terrier therefore had to be a strong, spirited dog to encourage the earth dweller to bolt and continue the chase. Although smaller than the fox, the terriers often knew the landscape and where the dens were. They could listen and figure out which den the fox might duck into and be there before the hounds by taking shortcuts. The intelligence of the terrier has always been notable when applied to hunting.

The Fox Terrier in the Show Ring

The popularity of the terriers reached its zenith in the late nineteenth century, and Fox Terriers were accepted as an English Kennel Club breed. Popular fashion tends to require change, and it was not long before the Fox Terrier was caught up in the whims of the show ring.

The breed developed an upright scapula (shoulder blade), a deepened chest, and a lengthened, narrowed head. In the show ring a smooth coat was favored over the less popular but more protective wiry-haired coat (rough or broken coat). The show ring's Fox Terrier was no longer at all like the working terriers in the hunt kennels. With its redesigned structure, it could not enter shallow earth even if the instinct to do so remained.

Russell himself was a member of England's Kennel Club (he was one of the original founders in 1873, and judged Fox Terriers at the first sanctioned show in 1874), but he did not exhibit his own dogs. Apparently disapproving of the changes in the terriers, he stated: "True terriers they were, but differing from the present show dogs as the wild eglantine differs from a garden rose."

The Working Terrier

As the popular Fox Terrier went to the shows, John Russell and other working terrier men went into the fields and followed hounds in pursuit of quarry. Many a man lacking wealth or a fine horse would nevertheless keep a few terriers to hunt when they were not hard at work. The ability of a good working dog to afford a man some sport locating fox or badger meant more than any pedigree. With the limited transportation available in those days, the terriers were rather closely bred. The best local working dogs were bred to local bitches, and definite types began to develop region by region, with size and temperament suitable to the area. All of these types were called "hunt" or "fox" terriers.

These working terriers have also been residents of stables for many years. Many are very adept at hunting vermin. The characteristics of gameness, hardiness, and intelligence have shaped this dog to several jobs over the years. Sometimes other breeds were crossed for the necessities of the work or terrain the terrier was applied to. But always the dog had to remain a small dog able to enter an earthen den and game enough to want to. The Jack Russell Terrier remained at work, and the show ring terrier became known as the Fox Terrier.

The Reverend Jack Russell

John Russell's dogs were of a type suitable to the terrain of the West Country where they lived. But, with the fame of both Reverend Russell and his dogs spreading, it became the desirable thing in other parts of the country to have one of his terriers. Apart from his church activities, the reverend was well known throughout England as a man passionate for the sport of fox hunting and breeding fox hunting dogs. Before long, the name Jack Russell Terrier spread and began to be applied to these feisty little working terriers.

The reverend's foundation bitch was named Trump. In 1819, while still an undergraduate at Oxford University, he bought her from a milkman in the Oxfordshire village of Marston. In Russell's eyes, Trump was the ideal terrier. She was white with brown ears, a patch of brown over each eye, and one no larger than a British penny at the base of her tail. Her coat was reported to be thick, close, and wiry, but not the long jacket of the Scottish terrier. Her legs were as straight as arrows, her feet were perfect, and she was of a size that has been compared to a grown vixen. Said Russell of this lovely animal: "Her whole appearance gave indications of courage, endurance and hardihood." Even now, there is a painting of Trump hanging in the harness room of the royal residence at Sandringham, in Norfolk, England.

Rev. Jack Russell's original kennels—this is where the Jack Russell Terrier began. These kennels were built from rock left over from the building of the railroad bed, and were located about 200 feet from the back of his home.

In England, the red fox was considered a varmint, a killer of spring lambs and poultry, so if the hunt crossed a farmer's land, risking damage to crops and fences, it was considered appropriate to kill the plentiful foxes encountered during the hunt. In America, there is little, if any, interest in harvesting foxes. Americans concentrate on the chase, and the greatest admirers of the fox are those who have spent time observing them and their intelligent strategies. Foxes in the country have many safe escape routes and seem to exhibit a sense of humor about the hounds "singing" their scent. Country sport affords a participant the pleasure of the sights and sounds of good hound work, and the enjoyment of following the hounds on horseback.

It has been reported that John Russell was also not interested in the killing of the fox. He said of the terriers: "A real Fox Terrier is not meant to murder and his intelligence should always keep him from such a crime." When fair terrier work is possible, with a noncombative terrier employed, one can well understand John Russell's fondness for the chase alone. He was a participant well into his 80s.

Russell became vicar of Swymbridge in 1832 and was occupied by both his church duties and his position as Master of Foxhounds. His circle of friends included the Prince of Wales (later King Edward VII) and other Masters of Foxhounds and often, even late in his life, he would travel long distances on horseback to meets. Legend has it that the bishop of his diocese once accused him of refusing to bury a body on a Wednesday because it interfered with the hunt. There are also stories of the bishop repeatedly asking Russell to give up his hounds and hunting. He agreed to give up his hounds. "Mrs. Russell shall keep them," he said.

After Jack Russell

Upon Jack Russell's death, at the age of 88, his stock was scattered. It is doubtful that anyone today can trace a terrier back to Trump.

What does live on is his strain or type of hardy, old-fashioned, willing-to-work terriers. Those who did not hunt were culled along the way, or kept as pets in homes of nonsporting people. Others who did not conform correctly for earth work, perhaps having too much blood of other breeds, were kept by people who found they were useful above ground for the task of rodent control. Some of these dogs had short, bandy legs and barrel chests. They may have carried some Dachshund or Bull Terrier blood.

Many of these pet strains came to the United States with fanciers who brought them from England. With them also came fine examples of the hardy, well-conformed working terrier so favored by the Reverend Russell himself. Fortunately, while the show-ring Fox Terrier continued to develop—and change—devoted

Although Trump's bloodlines have not survived, the ideal of the hardy, old-fashioned, willing-to-work terrier that she embodied lives on in the JRT.

fans of the original Fox Terrier continued to happily breed and work their tough little dogs in both Britain and North America. During this time they were still called by many names: hunt terrier, white terrier (after their extinct ancestor), and working Fox Terrier.

But as Greg Mousley, a noted terrier man and world authority on Jack Russell Terriers, relates, "Parson Russell was an extrovert and a flamboyant character and in his role as the sporting Parson he became very well known. Along with his fame went the awareness of his terriers, and when the Fox Terrier Club was formed, a name was needed for the many thousands of white bodied working terriers belonging to the working terriermen of the day, in order to distinguish them from their Kennel Club counterparts." They became known as Jack Russell Terriers.

JRTs in America

The Jack Russell Terrier Club of America (JRTCA) was founded in 1976. Thirty years later, thousands of members are united in admiration of and dedication to the protection of the Jack Russell Terrier.

The history of the Fox Terrier and the Jack Russell Terrier seems to have repeated itself when the Jack Russell Terrier Association of America (JRTAA)

What Is the Jack Russell Terrier Club of America?

The JRTCA is the largest breed club in the world dedicated to the Jack Russell Terrier. It is opposed to kennel club recognition of the breed and has a breed standard and a unique registry that allows registration only of adult dogs who are reviewed by a veterinarian for soundness and are found to be free of detectable defects. The JRTCA sanctions judges for the canine sports it supports, including conformation, go-to-ground, racing, and field work.

The JRTCA is also an educational organization dedicated to the motto "Preserve, Protect, and Work." It has an associated Research Foundation (www.jrt-research.com) that encourages, promotes, and supports research on genetic defects found in Jack Russells. It also supports Russell Rescue Inc. (www.russellrescue.com), a group that places abandoned, good-natured, healthy Jack Russells in permanent homes.

broke away from the JRTCA, with the intention of seeking recognition for the breed from the American Kennel Club. The Jack Russell Terrier was recognized by the United Kennel Club in 1991 and by the American Kennel Club in 1997—two moves that were opposed by the JRTCA.

Why do most of the Jack Russell Terrier clubs and the Jack Russell Terrier United World Federation oppose recognition by any all-breed kennel club? Why does the Jack Russell need "protection"? Showing dogs in highly competitive conformation contests has resulted in physical and mental changes to nearly every breed in history. While this kind of competition may be fine for other breeds, it is not suitable for the Jack Russell because beauty alone has nothing to do with the dog's ability to perform the task she was bred to do.

The Parson Russell Terrier

The JRTCA breed standard has not changed since the club was formed. But the little terriers being shown in AKC breed rings began to change—much as the Fox Terriers of old began to diverge from the working terriers in Britain. The

JRTCA eventually sold the name Parson Russell Terrier to the JRTAA. The idea was to help make clear the difference between the two breeds. In 2003 the AKC officially changed the breed name of the dogs it registers to the Parson Russell Terrier and the club changed its name to the Parson Russell Terrier Association of America.

With a more rigid standard that seems to place appearance above working ability, changes will happen quite quickly to this new terrier breed. The Parson Russell Terrier is already a dog of more substance than the Jack Russell Terrier. The Parson Russell standard tolerates less variation in height—just twelve to fourteen inches at the withers, compared to ten to fifteen inches for the Jack Russell, which is suitable for a variety of hunting applications. The Parson Russell breed standard notes a preference for a spot at the base of the tail, which will have some breeders working hard to breed dogs with those markings, rather than on striving to maintain the essence of what the dog should be, a working hunting terrier.

There is currently another group approaching the AKC with another variant of the breed that has short legs, again seeking to use the name Jack Russell Terrier. David Ross of the JRTCA comments, "By adopting the name 'Parson

The JRTCA sponsors events that give the Jack Russell an opportunity to do the work she was bred to do. In this go-to-ground competition, the dog (at the end of the tunnel) has found the quarry (which is protected in the round wire cage).

Russell Terrier' for the AKC variant of the Jack Russell Terrier, the AKC and the Jack Russell Terrier Association did in fact separate the standards into two different terriers, eliminating much of the confusion and leaving the name Jack Russell Terrier for the standard the JRTCA and the Jack Russell Terrier Club of Great Britain have used for many decades. While education and time will be needed for both our organizations to completely sort these terriers out in the public's mind, a good start has been made. However, if the AKC now accepts yet another standard for 'Short' Jack Russells and calls them 'Jack Russell Terrier,' both our registries will be in the unenviable position of telling innocent buyers that while their breeder and pedigree say they own a Jack Russell Terrier, the fact is they have purchased a 'new' variant of the terrier named after our terrier."

Preserving the Breed

The Fox Terrier was once the dog now known as the Jack Russell Terrier. However, today's Fox Terrier no longer has the conformational structure or even the desire to perform her original function of holding at bay or bolting foxes from their earth dens. The Jack Russell Terrier today is the unspoiled working terrier of the 1800s. The breed has been preserved in the standards of most of the major terrier clubs, which emphasize working ability. The mental and physical soundness of the Jack Russell Terrier is protected by those dedicated to their breed's performance and character.

Fierce protection of these traits motivates loyalty to the breed, and the members of the JRTCA are devoted to the organization and its task. Through understanding, the club can continue protecting this remarkable terrier.

Today, the Jack Russell is a much-loved pet in homes and families across the country. In addition to preserving the working function of the Jack Russell Terrier, the JRTCA educates pet owners about the unique qualities and requirements of keeping a Jack Russell. The JRTCA offers services and activities to keep people working and bonding with these special dogs. The club encourages people to love, play with, and work their terriers, and to fight for the dog's ability and instinct to work, both now and in the future.

Chapter 3

Why Choose a Jack Russell Terrier?

Choosing any breed of dog requires serious study of the attributes and behavior inherent in that breed. JRTs have become enormously popular, but the real Jack Russell Terrier may be very different from the dog you have seen on television or in the movies. That's why it's wise to get acquainted with a Jack Russell before you choose one.

They can be brave beyond belief and yet snuggly beyond compare. They can be brimming with love and affection, while at the same time they're a power-packed bundle of energy. A Jack Russell will make you laugh. Some will "hunt" the vacuum cleaner and try to grab it when you run it. They may pause at the top of an A-frame while doing agility just to take a look at their kingdom from that elevated viewpoint. They love the spotlight and thrive on your attention.

Because Jack Russells are compact in size, they make great traveling companions. A crate-trained Jack Russell can be taken many places where it would be harder to take a large dog. They enjoy riding in cars, too. Never leave the window open wide enough for a leap, though.

The only thing a JRT loves as much as being near you is going hunting. He may be glued to your side one moment and off on a mission the next. While a sense of humor is universal in the breed, when JRTs are hunting they are all business. They can change gears in a second from play to work.

Most the time, though, the Jack Russell is a comedian. Being playful and fun is part of his basic makeup. These are happy, cheerful dogs. But it is important to keep in mind that, besides being ready for fun, the entire wiring of the dog is

You will find your Jack Russell has a great sense of humor.

based on his history as a hunting dog. The dog must be willing to be handled and be a cheerful companion to the hunter. A dog of disagreeable nature would not be useful in the field.

Not an Apartment Dog

Because the JRT is small and very cute, many have been brought into small city apartments and condos and left alone while people work all day. The restrictions of being left alone in a confined place all day has made for some surprised owners, who come home to find their apartment ransacked by the bored dog. If left to entertain themselves, JRTs can be very busy doing things humans don't like. That havoc is very entertaining to the dog, though.

This is not a dog who can be crated for long hours and left alone. It is, in fact, cruel to crate a JRT for more than an hour or two. They do not thrive with such restrictions to their physical need for lots of exercise and their mental requirement to engage their minds in interesting activity.

Because of their enormous need for activity, Jack Russell Terriers are often misunderstood and even rejected. They can easily become unruly without good human leadership. Confused owners unprepared for the needs of the dog sometimes seek to place them with rescue groups or surrender them to shelters when they can no longer cope.

The Dog's Senses

The dog's eyes are designed so that he can see well in relative darkness, has excellent peripheral vision, and is very good at tracking moving objects, all skills that are important to a carnivore. Dogs also have good depth perception. Those advantages come at a price, though: Dogs are nearsighted and are slow to change the focus of their vision. It's a myth that dogs are color-blind. However, while they can see some (but not all) colors, their eyes were designed to most clearly perceive subtle shades of gray, an advantage when they are hunting in low light.

Dogs have about six times fewer taste buds on their tongue than humans do. They can taste sweet, sour, bitter, and salty tastes, but with so few taste buds than we do, they are likely to try anything and usually do.

A dog's ears can swivel independently, like radar dishes, to pick up sounds and pinpoint their location. Dogs can locate a sound in $6/100$ of a second and hear sound four times farther away than we can (which is why there is no reason to yell at your dog). They can also hear sounds at far higher pitches than we can.

In their first few days of life, puppies primarily use their sense of touch to navigate their world. Whiskers on the face, above the eyes, and below the jaws are sensitive enough to detect changes in airflow. Dogs also have touch-sensitive nerve endings all over their bodies, including on their paws.

Smell may be a dog's most remarkable sense. Dogs have about 220 million scent receptors in their nose, compared to about 5 million in humans, and a large part of the canine brain is devoted to interpreting scent. Not only can dogs smell scents that are very faint, but they can also accurately distinguish between those scents. In other words, when you smell a pot of spaghetti sauce cooking, your dog probably smells tomatoes and onions and garlic and oregano and whatever else is in the pot.

It is extremely important to be prepared for the basic characteristics and personality of *any* breed before getting one. People often spend more time selecting a pair of shoes than they do a companion animal that they will share their lives with for up to twenty years.

With his boundless energy, the Jack Russell is a challenge not everyone is prepared to provide for or cope with. Not all dog owners are up to the task of living with such a bold, devil-may-care breed.

Courageous and Reckless

If you can commit time and attention to a devoted, quick, intelligent companion, then the Jack Russell Terrier may fit into your life. You may find you are the dog's pet. It is quite like having a child in that you must devote a great deal of attention to where the dog is and what he is doing any given moment. A Jack Russell is brave to the point of abandon, and you must prevent him from self-destructing; more JRTs die from accidental deaths than from old age. If protected from themselves, they can live to be 20 years old. But you take on the job as the human parent to this clever, sometimes devilish companion.

Jack Russells need patient, vigilant guidance whenever they are awake. In a split second they have been known to bolt out of a door and across a road. If they spot a chipmunk or a squirrel, no amount of calling will get them to stop. They never see the trucks coming—they only see the object of their attention. No amount of obedience training will ever guarantee this dog's obedience. They have selective hearing and can completely ignore you. Heartbreak may be the result if you take chances.

It is always prudent to keep a Jack Russell on a leash in any situation where you could possibly lose control of the dog. Somehow they have such a spirit of adventure that their fearless nature compels many to make a bold leap into impending disaster without a split second of hesitation. There are many cases of Jack Russells leaping out of car windows at high speed. Heaven only knows why! I was on a lake one day when one of my own Jack Russell Terriers leaped out of the boat in the middle of the lake. He was rescued from the deep water with a fishing net. I do not know why my dog Cricketson jumped out of the boat. No way could that dog have swum to shore!

It is if Jack Russells are shooting stars with a brilliant light that shines through life, never looking back. They leave people who loved them in amazement and sorrow as they jump into danger's gaping jaws without fear or hesitation. It is desperately hard for those of us who love them to know why this self-destructive element is so strong in them. But when they decide they want to pursue some course of action, they are willing to do just about anything. That is why we must protect them so vigilantly from themselves.

These courageous, energetic dogs need supervised outlets for their endless energy.

Two Jack Russells?

The Jack Russell's willful ways require patient and loving guidance. Some owners get the idea that if they get two, the dogs will entertain each other. Two JRTs can become very close and enjoy each other's company, but a Jack Russell may not get along with another breed or another JRT of the same sex.

They have steadfast friendships with some dogs and strong dislikes to other dogs. They are somewhat snobbish and take to their own better than to other breeds. In a large gathering of Jack Russells, it takes only one dog of another breed or another color to get them all protesting. The one exception is hounds, for whom Jack Russells have a built-in respect, perhaps because they have hunted with them for generations.

It is best to keep only two Jack Russells together, and they should be of opposite genders. They are inclined to fight, especially dogs of the same sex, and if they do there will be no peace. When two females square off, the enmity between them can be to the death. Even catching the scent of the dog they dislike can raise their hackles in anticipation of a battle. Many owners report having to keep one dog crated or in a kennel while the other dog is out. Their politics are very complicated and baffled owners often have no idea why the sudden animosity has hatched. One thing is for sure, though: There is no cure. I offer this advice because the appeal of the Jack Russell makes one inclined to have more than one. Managing a pack of Jack Russells is a lot like taking preschoolers to the ballet.

Jack Russell Puppies

The Jack Russell puppy goes through an alligator stage where the entire world is centered in his mouth and those tiny sharp teeth. Expect puppies to be very active with their mouths. Teething may make the dog mouthy, too.

They normally play roughly and practice "killing" socks or toys. This behavior is completely normal. If you walk by, they may grab your pant leg and pretend they have caught you. It can be very funny, but do limit and discourage any really rough play. Do not encourage aggressive behavior. It may be cute when they are puppies, but it won't be cute later.

They can be terrible teenagers, too, but they soon mature. Keeping a Jack Russell well exercised is the best way to control this behavior. In fact, most behavior problems can be handled by extensive exercise. Exercise can help soften their zealous nature and single-mindedness.

Be gently forgiving of puppies playing like big hunting dogs. It is amazing to see the instincts present in a little dog only weeks old!

Other Pets

If you have other small pets, you must know that gerbils, birds, and even reptiles become the objects of the Jack Russell's compulsion to hunt. Any small pet may become the focus of the dog's unwavering attention. These dogs will give up sleep to focus on the pet. Their strong hunting instinct is ready and loaded.

As a rule, Jack Russells are not good companions with cats. Very few can ever fully be trusted with cats. Even when a dog is raised with a cat, the day may come that is not a happy one for the cat. No domestic animal more resembles the fox than a cat. The Jack Russell will decide to hunt the cat just as eagerly as his ancestors hunted fox.

A Jack Russell and chickens is about the most hopeless combination of animals there can be. The motion and squawking put the dog on overload.

Not long ago, my next-door neighbor had surgery, so his nephew kept his Jack Russell, Buckeye, for a few days while his uncle was in the hospital. Buckeye had been mannerly around our chickens. But during his stay with the nephew, he met a talking parrot. As the bird flew off his perch to land on the shoulder of the nephew, Buckeye jumped up and caught the bird in midair in front of horrified children and the woman who had patiently taught the bird to talk.

This breed possesses prey drive and simply cannot resist the opportunity to be full of surprises—not all of them good. They are adept at catching things, and sometimes they just cannot remember or recognize the limits of the game. They write their own rules to suit the moment.

Thriving on Praise

Most Jack Russells seek approval. They will go to great lengths to win praise. They so want attention that their behavior can mostly be shaped favorably with praise and rewards. They thrive on praise and do not take punishment well. Training them successfully means using positive forms and never harsh methods.

If they are not given approval, some may misbehave to get your full attention. Jack Russells do not like to be ignored. They so want to be liked that somehow when entering a room of people they will target the one person who is not interested in them and try to win them over. They will turn themselves inside out to be loved and to love back.

They are very sensitive to the moods of their owners. They seem to sense your feelings and will snuggle or lick a hand as if to console and extend understanding. They generally want to be in contact with your body or quite close. As I write, my young dog Twister either is under my chair or resting his head on my foot.

Your dog seeks your love and approval. Give him both, and he will be an amazing companion.

Chapter 4

Choosing Your Jack Russell Terrier

Now that you have researched the breed and feel sure you have the time and energy for a Jack Russell Terrier, it's time to find a reputable breeder. Buying a dog from a serious breeder is the best way to get a dog somebody has cared enough to breed to be the best they possibly can. A reputable breeder will take great care to bring puppies into the world who are healthy and well cared for from the beginning. A reputable breeder is more apt to aim to breed dogs without known defects.

JRTCA Breeders

The Jack Russell Terrier Club of America (JRTA) has one of the most unique registries in the world. It was set up by founder Alisia Crawford in 1976 specifically to protect the working terrier from genetic faults and structural characteristics that would be detrimental to the breed's working ability and mental and physical health.

Unlike other registries, such as the American Kennel Club and United Kennel Club, which register entire litters at birth, each application for registration for a Jack Russell Terrier is considered on the merits of each individual dog when she is 1 year old. That means just because a dog comes from registered parents does not mean she will be registered. A dog at 1 year must be examined by a veterinarian, and the doctor must note any obvious defects on a form submitted with the registration application.

Inbreeding is highly discouraged. Father to daughter, mother to son, and brother to sister matings are strictly prohibited, because inbreeding and line breeding can lead to increased risk of serious heritable diseases and traits. These defects would be detrimental to the future health of the working JRT.

A breeder who is a signatory of the JRTCA's Code of Ethics has contracted to uphold the club's high standards of conduct. Everything in the Code of Ethics is there to protect the dog and the well-being of the breed. All breeding stock must

A reputable breeder cares deeply about the future of the breed.

be registered and kept under clean and sanitary conditions. The puppies are required to be with their littermates and dam until they are at least 8 weeks old.

A reputable breeder, who is a caring guardian of the future and soundness of the breed, will be more apt to produce sound, healthy puppies. By selecting a soundly bred dog, you can better be protected from the later heartache of discovering your dog has serious health problems that could have been prevented by careful and thoughtful breeding.

How do you find a reputable breeder? The first step is to get in touch with as many breeders as possible in your area and arrange a visit for the whole family. The Jack Russell Terrier Club of America has breeder referral resources (you'll find their contact information in the appendix). If you have friends or neighbors who have healthy, well-behaved JRTs, you might want to ask them who the breeder was. You can also attend JRTCA events to meet Jack Russell breeders.

What to Look For

If at all possible, arrange to visit the breeder's kennel. You will better know the relationship the breeder has with their dogs if you visit. You will get to see firsthand how the dogs are kept and cared for. You want dogs who are well kept in clean conditions and looked after by loving keepers. If you can visit the litter, ask also to meet the dam and the stud dog if he is on the premises. Meet as many dogs in the puppy's pedigree as you can while visiting. Reputable breeders will be proud of their dogs and happy you want to meet the other dogs.

You will want a puppy who has been raised in the breeder's home, with lots of activity and contact with people and the normal sounds of a home. A puppy who

The Right Age to Leave Home

Any Jack Russell Terrier puppy should be allowed to stay with their dam and littermates for a full eight weeks. Some breeders keep pups a little longer. The pups are learning valuable lessons that they cannot get anywhere else in their lives. If denied, this time and learning can never be regained. The dam is teaching the pups, and they are teaching one another. These beginning lessons give the dog an important foundation for life. A reputable breeder wants their puppies to have a good start, and to be a good pet and companion to you. A happy healthy pet comes from a good beginning.

has been introduced to gentle children is more apt to love children and more inclined to be more patient with them.

When you visit, here are some questions to ask the breeder and points to consider:

- The breeder's house and surrounding area should be well kept up and clean.
- There should be no doggy smell when you enter the house.
- Ask if it is possible to meet all the dogs. The dogs should be friendly enough to happily receive visitors.
- Do the dogs have the run of the house? If not, can you actually visit the rooms they live in? This will tell you a lot about the environment in which they are raised.
- Are all the dogs happy and sociable?
- Are the dogs well groomed?
- Have the sire and the dam of the litter had health checks for genetic disease?
- Does the breeder BAER and CERF test his breeding stock? The BAER test scientifically proves the dog can hear, and the CERF test is to make sure the dog's eyes are in good health and clear. The BAER test need only be one time in the dog's life. The CERF test should be done yearly on dogs used for breeding.
- Does the breeder have a purchase contract?
- What kind of health guarantee comes with a puppy?
- Are the breeder's adult dogs registered with the Jack Russell Terrier Club of America?

A serious breeder will probably interview you as carefully as you are checking out a possible puppy prospect. Good breeders want their dogs to have good permanent homes. They will have a contract that protects their dog and also protects you. Make sure the breeder is willing to answer any questions about your new puppy when the purchase has been made. Ask if there are any genetic problems that the breeder has seen in their litters. Find out if the breeder will be helpful if for any reason in the future you cannot keep your dog. Beware of any breeder who does not care deeply about the fate of a dog they have bred.

Good breeders want every dog they breed to end up in a permanent, loving home.

Jack Russell Rescue

Instead of a puppy, you might want to consider a recycled Jack Russell Terrier. Perfectly wonderful dogs sometimes have to find new homes. It is not any fault of the dog. Humans get ill or move where they cannot keep a pet. People get divorced and can no longer care for a pet.

Dogs who need homes are most often adults. They are spayed or neutered and housetrained. Russell Rescue Inc., the rescue organization associated with the JRTCA, screens all dogs and is very careful not to place any dogs with known behavior problems or serious health issues. Rescue also screens the homes these dogs go to. All adoptions are by application. (You'll find contact information in the appendix.)

Often rescue dogs go to foster homes before they are adopted, so the foster family learns a great deal about the dog in their care. You might enjoy being a foster home and eventually adopting a dog in your care. Rescues need foster homes as much as they need funds to carry out the work of rescue. All foster homes need containment for a dog and an understanding of the needs of the breed.

Some shelters and humane societies keep a list of people who apply to adopt a specific breed. Please know that Jack Russells do not fare well in shelters. Being in such unfamiliar surroundings and under such stress can make a Jack Russell behave uncharacteristically shy or aggressive toward the other dogs in holding runs. This makes JRTs tough to adopt out. Some shelters will not take Jack Russells because of their distress at being sheltered. They often are completely undone and fall apart in such circumstances. But that same unhappy dog in the shelter may be a happy dog if she is played with outside for an interview.

Dogs with a second chance for a home make wonderful, loving pets. Many rescued dogs seem to understand their good fortune and express great gratitude and affection to those who have chosen them. A rescued dog can give you boundless love, and you can do a dog a great service by giving her a second chance at life in a permanent home. The love you give and the love you will get back from a rescue dog is very satisfying. It is a win-win situation for both of you.

Where Not to Get a Jack Russell

Backyard breeders and pet shops are not the best places from which to get a dog, nor is someone breeding a litter so their children can see "the miracle of birth." These folks are not the best guardians of the breed.

Backyard Breeders

Backyard breeders are those who have bred their dogs but do not have the knowledge (or desire, or energy, or finances) to do what is necessary to produce the best dogs possible. This could be someone who has a female Jack Russell Terrier and wants puppies, and so breeds the female to a friend's male down the street. No health checks were done, no studies of genetics or background checks were done, and in many instances the dogs may not have been registered, either.

A backyard breeder may also be someone who hasn't spayed the female and then doesn't keep her safe when she comes into season and is bred by a wandering male. The puppies may or may not be purebred; the male (or males) may not even be known.

Most such people are not breeding for the future health and soundness of the breed. They have not looked over pedigrees and studied what stud dog would improve the qualities of their bitch and have not done all the appropriate homework and preparation for a litter of puppies. They likely have not had the bitch tested or even registered. Most such breedings are due to any convenient stud dog.

Why Not Buy from a Pet Store?

The only advantage to buying a JRT from a pet store is that you can have a puppy the day you walk in. There are many disadvantages. A pet store does not

When you get your dog from a reputable JRTCA breeder, the puppies must be kept with their mom and littermates until they are at least 8 weeks old.

sell adults or rehome abandoned dogs. Many times the pups are taken from their dam and littermates way too early for their well-being.

Pet shops frequently buy their puppies from commercial breeding facilities (sometimes known as puppy mills) where there is little thought or care for the well-being of the puppy. JRTs in puppy mills are generally not registered with the JRTCA and there may be no way of verifying their pedigree—if, indeed, a pedigree is offered. Most puppy mill dogs come without pedigrees.

You'll also pay a lot more than you would from a breeder, you won't be able to see where or how the dog was raised, you're unable to meet the dog's relatives to see if they are the kinds of dogs you would want to have, and you won't know the dog's health history. Pet store employees won't be able to show you how to groom your dog and won't be able to answer any questions you have as the years go by. And if you have to rehome the dog, a pet store will never take her back. A reputable breeder will.

Pet shops are selling Jack Russells strictly to make a profit. Dogs bred only for dollars are the worst possible choice.

Part II

Caring for Your
Jack Russell Terrier

Chapter 5

Bringing Home Your Jack Russell Terrier

With preparation and planning, your new dog's arrival will be a happy event. Jack Russells adjust very quickly to new situations and adapt themselves nicely to a new home.

If possible, visit your new puppy a time or two before bringing him home. (Check with the breeder first regarding his or her policy about visitors before the pups have had their first protective inoculations.) It is also good to meet the dam (mother) and the sire (father) to give you a better understanding of the personality and characteristics your dog may have.

For the first few days, try to keep visitors and activities to a minimum. Give your new family member a bit of time to become acclimated to his people and his surroundings.

Time to Shop

Rather than forget something or having to settle for what you don't really like, take your time shopping *before* you bring your puppy home and have his supplies ready. The basics are outlined in the box on page 43, but here are a few more things to consider.

Puppy Essentials

You'll need to go shopping *before* you bring your puppy home. There are many, many adorable and tempting items at pet supply stores, but these are the basics.

- **Food and water dishes.** Look for bowls that are wide and low or weighted in the bottom so they will be harder to tip over. Sturdy crock bowls are very good for JRTs. They are easy to clean (plastic never gets completely clean), difficult to tip over, and tough for your puppy to pick up and carry off to who-knows-where. Avoid bowls that place the food and water side by side in one unit—it's too easy for your dog to get his water dirty that way.
- **Leash.** A six-foot leather leash will be easy on your hands and very strong.
- **Collar.** Start with a nylon buckle collar. For a perfect fit, you should be able to insert two fingers between the collar and your pup's neck. Your dog will need larger collars as he grows up.
- **Crate.** Choose a sturdy crate that is easy to clean and large enough for your puppy to stand up, turn around, and lie down in.
- **Nail cutters.** Get a good, sharp pair that are the appropriate size for the nails you will be cutting. Your dog's breeder or veterinarian can give you some guidance here.
- **Grooming tools.** Different kinds of dogs need different kinds of grooming tools. See chapter 7 for advice on what to buy.
- **Chew toys.** Dogs *must* chew, especially puppies. Make sure you get things that won't break or crumble off in little bits, which the dog can choke on. Very hard plastic bones are a good choice. Dogs love rawhide bones, too, but pieces of the rawhide can get caught in your dog's throat, so they should only be allowed when you are there to supervise.
- **Toys.** Watch for sharp edges and unsafe items such as plastic eyes that can be swallowed. Many toys come with squeakers, which dogs can also tear out and swallow. All dogs will eventually destroy their toys; as each toy is torn apart, replace it with a new one.

*You'll need to do a lot of shopping **before** you bring your puppy home.*

Crate and Bed

You will need a crate, of course, with a pad and bedding inside. You might also want to get another small bed for use outside the crate. A bed that is his own will give your dog a feeling of well-being and security. If allowed to, JRTs will be happy to snuggle next to you in your bed or on the couch. Do make sure the dog always knows it is *your* bed, though, and that they must never be bossy while in your "lair." Some Jack Russells have a tendency to take over. Don't indulge the dog in behavior that may become troublesome later.

A particularly appealing bed for JRTs is a cup type made of sturdy, plush, washable material. Have a few soft, washable pads available so you can rotate them for washing as needed. Keep your puppy's crate and bed out of drafts and direct sunlight.

Leash and Collar

You will need a leash and a collar or collars that fit properly at all stages of growth. Rolled leather collars work very well and are comfortable. Be sure to adjust the collar so that it fits securely but not tightly, and check it regularly, particularly as your puppy grows. (The collar should be snug enough that it will not slip over the dog's head, but loose enough to allow you to comfortably insert two or three fingers between the collar and the neck.)

A nylon leash is often best for puppies, who find great joy in chewing leather leashes. A leash with a larger clip is much easier to get on a wiggling dog than one with a tiny clip. Make sure the clip is sturdy and will not release accidentally.

A retractable leash is good for walks in open areas. It allows the dog freedom, but you do give up some control. With a length of up to sixteen feet, instead of the six feet of most leashes, your dog will be harder to control. The retractable leash is never a substitute for the better control of a six-foot leash in areas where there are other dogs, cats, and people. You always need to keep your Jack Russell under control for safety. It's a challenge to assume control over a Jack Russell Terrier, with or without a leash!

Containment

You will not want to give a puppy free run of the house until he is housetrained. Even an older dog arriving into a new home may be excited and make mistakes. It is easier to keep the dog in a safe restricted area until the dog settles and relaxes. That means, in addition to the crate, you will need baby gates or some kind of portable pen so you can restrict your dog's freedom in the house.

Toys

Jack Russells love toys, and appropriate ones are necessary for all stages of their lives. Hard rubber or nylon toys are best, but soft rubber squeaky toys are not at all suitable. They are easily torn apart, and the squeaker is small enough for the dog to choke on. The soft rubber usually ends up shredded and swallowed.

Hard rubber balls are always a favorite, and the ones with a channel cut through them are easy for little mouths to carry. Rope toys with hard rubber chew areas are very suitable and come in many shapes and sizes. Just be careful you do not leave your dog working on any toy he can chew into dangerously small pieces.

Chew hooves are a good source of hours of chewing for a Jack Russell. Rawhide chew strips are favored by some, but do not offer the ones with the twisted ends. A dog can get the end pieces loose and choke to death on them.

Never give your dog an old shoe or slipper to chew on. He will not know the difference between the old shoe and your good shoes. In fact, never allow your puppy or dog to chew on anything that is not meant for that activity, and always be ready to provide him with a good toy as a substitute for whatever forbidden item might be in his mouth. In distracting the puppy from such negative behavior, be sure to praise him for accepting the substitution.

TIP

Rotate your dog's toys so he does not get bored.

Toys aren't just for little puppies. Dogs need appropriate toys all their lives.

Puppy-Proofing

You still have work to do before the big day to provide a safe environment. You will need to puppy proof your home to preserve both your dog and your sanity. The box on pages 48–49 explains puppy-proofing.

Curious busy little teeth on terriers have been known to chew up dentures, hearing aids, and eyeglasses. It is better to be safe and not leave anything with your scent on it that can be reached and chewed by your puppy or adult dog. They are little athletes and can get up on things to reach items that interest them.

If you bring a puppy or adult dog home in the summer, make sure he cannot accidentally get into a swimming pool. Lots of Jack Russells love water and swimming, but your dog should always do so under your supervision. When your dog is allowed to swim, install a safety ramp so he can get out of the pool without the danger of drowning.

Inspect your fence regularly. Make sure there are no gaps under, between, or through any part of the fence and that it is tall enough to contain a small dog who can jump several times his height. Because of their inquisitive nature, without attention to protection and good containment, JRTs can wander. Rather than risk your dog being picked up by animal control, and possibly not being reunited with you, keep him safely contained at home and safe on a leash when you're out.

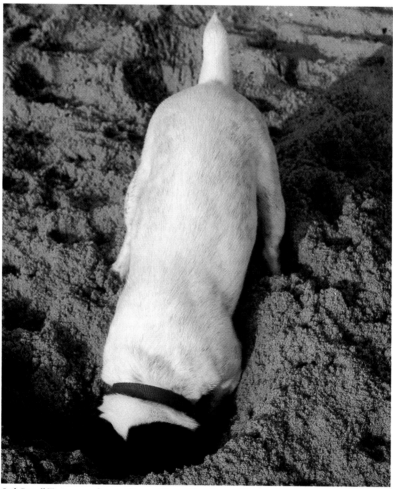

Jack Russell Terriers were born to dig—and jump. Your fence will have to be tall enough to contain your dog and sunk deep enough into the ground to foil his digging efforts.

The Big Day

Finally, the day has arrived to pick up your dog. Before you get the dog into your car, give him a chance to relieve himself. If the breeder has not taken your puppy for a car ride before, ask them to skip the pup's breakfast that day so he won't have an upset stomach in the car. Carry paper towels with you, just in case. Most Jack Russells learn very quickly to love riding in the car.

Puppy-Proofing Your Home

You can prevent much of the destruction puppies can cause and keep your new dog safe by looking at your home and yard from a dog's point of view. Get down on all fours and look around. Do you see loose electrical wires, cords dangling from the blinds, or chewy shoes on the floor? Your pup will see them too!

In the kitchen:

- Put all knives and other utensils away in drawers.
- Get a trash can with a tight-fitting lid.
- Put all household cleaners in cupboards that close securely; consider using childproof latches on the cabinet doors.

In the bathroom:

- Keep all household cleaners, medicines, vitamins, shampoos, bath products, perfumes, makeup, nail polish remover, and other personal products in cupboards that close securely; consider using childproof latches on the cabinet doors.
- Get a trash can with a tight-fitting lid.
- Don't use toilet bowl cleaners that release chemicals into the bowl every time you flush.
- Keep the toilet bowl lid down.
- Throw away potpourri and any solid air fresheners.

In the bedroom:

- Securely put away all potentially dangerous items, including medicines and medicine containers, vitamins and supplements, perfumes, and makeup.
- Put all your jewelry, barrettes, and hairpins in secure boxes.
- Pick up all socks, shoes, and other chewables.

In the rest of the house:

- Tape up or cover electrical cords; consider childproof covers for unused outlets.
- Knot or tie up any dangling cords from curtains, blinds, and the telephone.

- Securely put away all potentially dangerous items, including medicines and medicine containers, vitamins and supplements, cigarettes, cigars, pipes and pipe tobacco, pens, pencils, felt-tip markers, craft and sewing supplies, and laundry products.
- Put all houseplants out of reach.
- Move breakable items off low tables and shelves.
- Pick up all chewable items, including television and electronics remote controls, cell phones, shoes, socks, slippers and sandals, food, dishes, cups and utensils, toys, books and magazines, and anything else that can be chewed on.

In the garage:

- Store all gardening supplies and pool chemicals out of reach of the dog.
- Store all antifreeze, oil, and other car fluids securely, and clean up any spills by hosing them down for at least ten minutes.
- Put all dangerous substances on high shelves or in cupboards that close securely; consider using childproof latches on the cabinet doors.
- Pick up and put away all tools.
- Sweep the floor for nails and other small, sharp items.

In the yard:

- Put the gardening tools away after each use.
- Make sure the kids put away their toys when they're finished playing.
- Keep the pool covered or otherwise restrict your pup's access to it when you're not there to supervise.
- Secure the cords on backyard lights and other appliances.
- Inspect your fence thoroughly. If there are any gaps or holes in the fence, fix them.
- Make sure you have no toxic plants in the garden.

Be sure to get the paperwork and health records from the breeder, and some of the food the dog is used to eating. If the breeder provides you with the signed pedigree and required stud service certificate you will need when he is a year old to register him, keep those papers in a safe place so they are not lost.

Many JRTCA breeders will provide those papers when your dog is nearing a year for registration. You will need to join the JRTCA to register your dog (you'll find contact information in the appendix). There are many advantages to the membership and the ensuing kinship between Jack Russell lovers.

If you already have a dog at home, introduce the new dog (puppy or adult) on neutral territory, such as out on a walk at a park, keeping a brisk walk until they have observed each other and gotten the scent and attitude of the other dog. It is always good to introduce any two adult dogs this way to prevent any problems of dominance by just bringing a new dog into another dog's territory.

Crate Training

Jack Russells love their crates and use them as dens. When the door is left open and there is a comfortable bed inside, the dog will seek the crate for privacy and rest. Either a wire crate or a molded plastic carrier is suitable, as long as it is large enough for a grown Jack Russell to stand up in and turn around comfortably. If the crate is too large the dog may choose to sleep at one end and eliminate at the other.

The bed or pad inside should be one that is not easily torn. An added baby blanket will let a puppy snuggle in and will help provide warmth and protection from drafts, especially in cold weather. A crate should not be used for more than a few hours at a time and should never be used for punishment. The crate should be a safe and happy place for your dog—a place where he will go willingly, whether you put him there or he goes in of his own accord.

> **CAUTION**
>
> Collars with tags should be removed before crating the dog. Tags can become caught in the crate and the dog can be injured or strangled. They are best taken off in the kennel, too.

Where you place the crate in your home is important for your dog's comfort. Keep it out of drafts and direct sunlight (for a wire crate, a sheet or blanket can be used as a cover for privacy and draft protection, and removed when not needed). It is also very important that the crate be in a "people area," not in a place where the dog will be isolated from his family.

Choose a time to start crate training when the dog is ready for rest, after he has relieved himself and has had plenty of exercise. Start by feeding your dog in the crate with the door open. He will quickly associate the crate with this reward.

Now that he has been eating his meals in his crate, you can use a small treat and happy voice of encouragement, and add a command, and he will enter the crate. At first, just quietly close the door and don't latch it. Later, when he is comfortable with the door being swung shut and he is busy with a treat or a meal, latch the door a few minutes at a time. If he fusses, wait until he settles down to let him out.

Some JRT owners use an ex-pen to keep their dogs contained and safe in unfamiliar areas outdoors.

By offering him special treats and chew toys in the crate, he should not be upset by the door closing. Take these special crate toys and goodies away when he is not in the crate. When he is in the crate and occupied with a treat or special chew toy, leave the room quietly and return. Teach him this important lesson without discussion: When you leave, you always return.

Routine

A routine is helpful to all dogs. Upon rising, they need to relieve themselves and play, then go back to rest some more. After their morning nap, they are ready for more play and exercise, and then their afternoon nap. If you work at home, you have an ideal companion. If you work away from home, it is best if you can get back at midday to spend some time with the dog, let him out, and play with him. If your dog must be alone during the day, leave a radio on to keep him company and use gates to confine him to one or two rooms, but don't leave him by himself for too many hours, and never leave him crated for more than a few hours at a time. This is especially hard for puppies, who may feel they are being punished or abandoned.

> **TIP**
>
> Be sure to have a veterinarian and take your new puppy for a visit to acquaint the puppy with the vet. Many breeders suggest you have your new puppy examined by a vet, anyway, because you want to be sure your puppy or dog is off to the best possible start. Be sure to take the medical records from the breeder to your veterinarian.

Perhaps a friend or neighbor can help by spending some time with the dog in the early afternoon, as JRTs really do cherish companionship. If you have no alternative but to be gone all day, and no one to help, you might want to consider waiting and getting a dog or puppy at another time in your life.

When you get home, take the dog outside immediately and later, after feeding and watering, take him on a long evening walk.

Bringing Home an Adult Dog

In this chapter we have been focusing on bringing a Jack Russell puppy into your home, but this is not the only option. Consider getting an older, already spayed or neutered Jack Russell as companion to your dog—or as your only dog, for that matter. Many healthy, well-behaved older JRTs need new homes and can be applied for through the JRTCA's Russell Rescue (see the appendix).

An older dog entering your home and life for the first time will have different needs than a puppy. A new puppy adjusts easily and is more adaptable, but an older dog has a history and habits, and may be more cautious in his new surroundings. The best thing you can do is to make the homecoming as stress-free as possible and make your home a comfortable, stable environment in which your new dog will feel secure.

If you get a rehomed dog from a rescue group or other source, you may not know much about the dog's history. The more you can find out, the better prepared you will be for the task ahead. Unfortunately, some rescue dogs have been harmed by humans and will have to be patiently taught to love and trust again. Many foster homes work on helping the dog gain confidence and trust before placing him in a permanent home.

You can make this easier by being sensitive to the special circumstances of your JRT. Notice anything that seems to make him uncomfortable. Avoid movements or noises that seem to scare him. Introduce children to your new dog in as calm a manner as possible. Don't let them jump on him or make loud, excited noises that may startle or frighten him.

An adult JRT will quickly adjust to your home and your life, and will make a super companion.

Take your dog for long walks around your neighborhood to let him get his bearings and familiarize himself with his new environment. The sooner he feels at home, the better.

An older JRT should adjust quickly to your home and lifestyle. They are "no-regrets" dogs. With patience and understanding, he will soon be his happy, eager Jack Russell self. You can be proud you have offered him a second chance and a wonderful new home.

Chapter 6

Feeding Your Jack Russell Terrier

People have different opinions about the proper feeding of Jack Russell Terriers. All agree, however, that good nutrition is essential to good health, and that the nutritional needs of the dog change throughout her life.

Feeding Your Jack Russell Puppy

Having started life on mother's milk, puppies are weaned between five and six weeks of age. The timing depends on the dam's willingness to nurse and the practices of the breeder. While the pups are still nursing, at about four weeks, the breeder will begin to feed them a fine-textured, well-moistened, nutritious gruel to begin to accustom them to solid food. At first the food is all over the place. It must be served in a low dish or pan so the pups can reach it, but then, of course, they can also walk through and play in it. This milestone in the puppies' lives marks the beginning of several weeks of more cleanup work for the breeder.

Puppies should never leave their dam and littermates before they are 8 weeks of age, and by the time you bring your puppy home she will have been fully weaned and eagerly crunching on puppy kibble. The breeder should send you home with a supply of the food the pup has been eating. You can either continue feeding that food or change to a different one. If you change, do it gradually, starting with about 25 percent of the new food and gradually increasing the proportion for about a week until only the new food is being served. (Changing food for dogs of any age should be done in this gradual manner to avoid upsetting the puppy's or dog's digestive system.)

Young puppies should be fed three times a day, at about the same times each day. Offer one-third of the daily ration at each serving. Set the food down in front of the pup and allow her to eat for ten or fifteen minutes. At the end of that time, pick up the dish and do not offer more food until the next mealtime.

You probably won't have to worry about your Jack Russell puppy eating enough—most are eager eaters. They may play around or even miss a meal or two, particularly when they are first brought to their new home, but they will soon get with the program. (A loss of appetite for longer periods may require your veterinarian's attention.) Be very sure that plenty of fresh, clean water is always available.

Puppies require more protein and calories per pound of body weight than adults, so a general rule for Jack Russells is to serve the same amount of food per day to a pup as you would expect her to eat each day as an adult. For the most part, this would be about one cup of good-quality, small kibble per day. You can check with the breeder for information on how much food he or she expects your pup will require as an adult. Feeding guidelines printed on dog food bags are only estimates and should not be relied on as the precise amounts to feed your dog or puppy.

When your puppy reaches 5 or 6 months of age, she can be fed just twice a day, morning and evening, one-half the daily ration each time. Many breeders continue to feed two meals a day throughout the life of the dog, but some choose to feed only once a day after the dog reaches adulthood.

Puppies need more protein and calories per pound of body weight than adults.

Feeding the Older Jack Russell

Jack Russells remain quite active well into their senior years. However, compared to the activity levels they maintained as youngsters, even these lively terriers tend to slow down and nap more as they age, perhaps gaining some weight in the process.

When JRTs get to be more than 6 years old they may require fewer calories (particularly if they are gaining some weight), although they still need all of the essential nutritional elements found in a well-balanced food. As the metabolism also slows down a bit, you may want to feed your senior JRT smaller, more frequent meals.

An older Jack Russell may become a fussy eater. Have your veterinarian keep a close eye on the health of the teeth of your older Jack Russell. Teeth should be examined yearly to avoid any problems that may prevent the older dog from eating comfortably.

Free Feeding?

Free feeding (having food available for your dog at all times) is not recommended for Jack Russells—it is just too tempting. A fat Jack Russell Terrier is not desirable, nor is she healthy. JRTs should always be in good working condition.

All calories do count. Be sure to include biscuits and treats when calculating your dog's total daily intake. A good, quick way to determine if your Jack Russell is carrying too much fat is to put your hand over her back, thumb on one side, fingers on the other, and run your hand lightly down the back. You should be able to feel the individual ribs but you should not be able to see them.

> **TIP**
>
> **Feeding More than One**
>
> If you are feeding more than one puppy or dog, it is best to keep them separated, preferably serving them in their individual crates. That way, you will avoid conflict and you can be sure that each dog gets to eat her full portion. Remove any food that has not been eaten within ten or fifteen minutes.

What to Feed Your JRT

Dry food, or primarily dry food, is recommended. Some warm water may be added to kibble to release more food odors. Canned foods are not always necessary but, if you feel you must add them, take care that they do not exceed 20 or

Reading Dog Food Labels

Dog food labels are not always easy to read, but if you know what to look for they can tell you a lot about what your dog is eating.

- The label should have a statement saying the dog food meets or exceeds the American Association of Feed Control Officials (AAFCO) nutritional guidelines. If the dog food doesn't meet AAFCO guidelines, it can't be considered complete and balanced, and can cause nutritional deficiencies.
- The guaranteed analysis lists the minimum percentages of crude protein and crude fat and the maximum percentages of crude fiber and water. AAFCO requires a minimum of 18 percent crude protein for adult dogs and 22 percent crude protein for puppies on a dry matter basis (that means with the water removed; canned foods should have more protein because they have more water). Dog food must also have a minimum of 5 percent crude fat for adults and 8 percent crude fat for puppies.
- The ingredients list the most common item in the food first, and so on until you get to the least common item, which is listed last.
- Look for a dog food that lists an animal protein source first, such as chicken or poultry meal, beef or beef byproducts, and that has other protein sources listed among the top five ingredients. That's because a food that lists chicken, wheat, wheat gluten, corn, and wheat fiber as the first five ingredients has more chicken than wheat, but may not have more chicken than all the grain products put together.
- Other ingredients may include a carbohydrate source, fat, vitamins and minerals, preservatives, fiber, and sometimes other additives purported to be healthy.
- Some grocery store brands may add artificial colors, sugar, and fillers—all of which should be avoided.

25 percent of the dog's diet. A puppy raised on dry food, with or without the occasional addition of water, will be quite content with that food for her lifetime.

To help keep your dog's teeth and gums healthy, avoid semimoist food (which has a lot of salt, sugar, and preservatives) and too much canned food. These soft preparations encourage tartar buildup, which can lead to periodontal disease. Hard kibble helps keep teeth clean and gums healthy.

JRTs do not need to have food available all the time, but they do always need access to fresh, clean water.

There are so many brands and types of dog food, it can be difficult to decide what is best for your Jack Russell. Premium, high-quality food should always be chosen over less expensive food that may contain poor-quality ingredients, fillers, and artificial colors and additives.

The dog's stool is a primary indicator of the digestibility (usable amount of nutrients) of the food she is eating. Lower-cost foods may be soy- or corn-based, which tends to produce a larger, looser stool. A food that is based on good animal proteins will produce a firm, well-formed stool.

Although store and discount brands should probably be avoided, relatively low-cost, high-quality foods are still available in grocery, feed, and specialty stores. Read and compare labels (see the box on page 57), seek quality and palatability, and you can be sure that you will be providing the best food available for your dog.

Protein

One area of debate about canine nutrition involves protein. Some people believe that if some is good, more is better, particularly for puppies and bitches who are pregnant or lactating. But high concentrations of protein in a dog's diet are believed to be hard on the kidneys, especially for dogs with a history of kidney problems. Working dogs and puppies may be fed food with protein levels of 25 or 26 percent; mature dogs fare well with a level of 20 percent.

Fat

Another consideration is the fat content of dog food. Owners of working dogs and dogs housed in outdoor kennels in cold weather may prefer a higher fat content, maybe 15 percent. Dogs, and even puppies, who are housed indoors, and older and overweight dogs will probably do very well on a food with a fat content of around 10 percent.

Supplements

One more consideration is supplements. Don't give them unless your veterinarian prescribes them for some special reason. All good-quality dog foods labeled as "complete" will provide all that your dog needs in the way of nutrition. There may be rare or special circumstances, such as pregnancy and lactation, when your dog requires some supplementation of one or more nutrients, if recommended by your veterinarian. But casual supplementation can cause serious imbalances and unexpected problems. More of a good thing is not necessarily better.

Basically, the food you serve your Jack Russell Terrier should contain protein, fat, carbohydrates, fiber, vitamins, and minerals, all in proper quantities and in proper proportions. It is highly unlikely that a high-quality food will be lacking in any nutrient your dog needs for healthy growth, development, and maintenance.

It is impossible to give general advice and be right all the time. You know your Jack Russell Terrier better than anyone else. As a responsible pet owner, you should seek the advice of your veterinarian and the dog's breeder, read labels, and then decide what food is best. The appearance of your dog is the best indicator of good nutrition; watch her as she develops, grows, and ages, and adjust her diet accordingly.

Snacks

Just like adding artificial colors to dog food, feeding table scraps does more to please people than to benefit dogs. Your dog doesn't care about all those flavors and colors. She's perfectly happy with that plain old high-quality kibble she's always eaten. And if you never feed her table scraps, she'll never know what she's missing.

Scraps tend to be full of fat, salt, sugar, and spices—nothing that's needed by or is good for your dog.

Carrots are a healthy snack for your dog.

Pet Food vs. People Food

Many of the foods we eat are excellent sources of nutrients—after all, we do just fine on them. But dogs, just like us, need the right combination of meat and other ingredients for a complete and balanced diet, and a bowl of meat doesn't provide that. In the wild, dogs eat the fur, skin, bones, and guts of their prey, and even the contents of the stomach.

This doesn't mean your dog can't eat what you eat. A little meat, dairy, bread, some fruits, or vegetables as a treat are great. Just remember, we're talking about the same food you eat, not the gristly, greasy leftovers you would normally toss in the trash. Stay away from sugar, too, and remember that chocolate is toxic to dogs.

If you want to share your food with your dog, be sure the total amount you give her each day doesn't make up more than 15 percent of her diet, and that the rest of what you feed her is a top-quality complete and balanced dog food. (More people food could upset the balance of nutrients in the commercial food.)

Can your dog eat an entirely homemade diet? Certainly, if you are willing to work at it. Any homemade diet will have to be carefully balanced, with all the right nutrients in just the right amounts. It requires a lot of research to make a proper homemade diet, but it can be done. It's best to work with a veterinary nutritionist.

Even if you feed something healthy from the table, the dog will still get into the habit of begging, which will become a mealtime annoyance forever—not to mention the fact that your JRT could end up being a very finicky eater.

Good people food snacks for your dog, in moderation, are pieces of carrot or apple. Most JRTs love them. Offer the snacks between meals—yours and the dog's—or as rewards in training sessions.

Never feed your dog cooked bones as they splinter and can perforate the intestines. And never feed small, sharp bones to your dog. The best bones to feed are the leg bones of cows. Don't overdo it, though, because too much bone chewing can cause extreme wear on a mature dog's teeth.

Chapter 7

Grooming Your Jack Russell Terrier

Although the Jack Russell Terrier is considered a no-frills kind of dog, all working terriers need their coats maintained to keep them efficient and neat. Weekly maintenance of the Jack Russell Terrier's coat will give you a chance to look your dog over carefully and make sure all is in good order.

This chapter outlines procedures for the thorough care and grooming of your JRT's coat. However, the average dog will do just as well with basic grooming, together with proper care of the nails and feet and attention to health matters.

The real object is to get your hands on your dog daily or, at the very least, weekly. Doing this, you will have an opportunity to bond with your dog while giving him a thorough health inspection. Make it a really fun time for both of you. Your dog will come away looking and feeling his best, and you will have the satisfaction of knowing you are taking the best possible care of him.

The Jack Russell Coat

The Jack Russell is a double-coated breed, which means he has a dense under-coat with a harsh overcoat that will protect him from the elements and the underbrush. The coat comes in three varieties: smooth, broken, and rough. Smooth coats shed more freely than the rough or broken coats, but if you are uncomfortable finding white hairs year round on your clothing and furniture, be warned that this is unavoidable with a Jack Russell in your home.

Basic Supplies

Here's what you will need to groom your JRT:

- Bristle brush
- Grooming scissors
- Horsehair glove
- Magnet cloth
- Stripping knives, fine and coarse
- Metal flea comb
- Nail trimmer
- Rubber hound glove
- Thinning scissors
- Trimmer knife
- Styptic powder
- Volcanic rock

To begin grooming your dog, place him on a table set at a height that will make the dog easy to work with and that is comfortable for your back. A professional grooming table is easiest for this purpose; it's adjustable, has a nonskid surface, and comes with an extendable arm from which hangs a loop of leash (known as a noose) that you can use to keep your hands free for grooming. Never leave the dog unattended for even a second while he is restrained in the noose. If you must stop grooming, have a crate ready in which to place the dog until you return.

Grooming a Smooth-Coated JRT

For a smooth-coated JRT, start with a thorough, all-over brushing, followed by a rubdown with a well-soaked, tightly squeezed magnet cloth A magnet cloth (or, as it is sometimes called, a "magic magnet cloth") is used for its ability to absorb and hold water. It is often yellow and is made of a washable cloth fiber that can be washed over and over again but not machine dried. Equine or tack stores often sell them for polishing horse's coats. Some dog supply catalogs offer them in the grooming section. The cloth removes old hair and debris, giving a nice fresh look to the coat.

Then look the dog over for anything that may need attention: teeth, eyes, nails, injury to the foot pads, fleas and ticks (comb him through with the metal flea comb for a thorough check), an unusual smell in the ears, and so forth. (Any unusual smell or matter in the ears requires the attention of a veterinarian.) Follow this routine weekly.

You will also want to brush the dog almost daily because the smooth coat sheds so freely. During the shedding season in spring and fall, take your dog outside to groom him. You can use a bristle brush to remove loose hairs so your home is less filled with the cactuslike hairs of the Jack Russell.

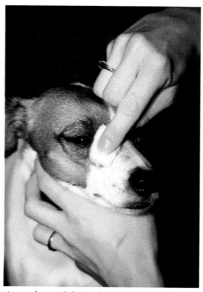

A smooth-coated dog needs regular brushing. Remember to clean his eyes and ears every time you groom him.

Grooming a Rough- or Broken-Coated JRT

Rough or broken-coated JRTs require a bit more work. Left to grow naturally, the coat may not look neat and tidy. Although grooming the roughs or brokens is more involved, you may derive more satisfaction from the finished product.

Always keep in mind the Jack Russell is a double-coated breed: He has an undercoat and an overcoat. The overcoat is made up of the coarser hairs that protect the dog from briars and brush in the field.

Begin by thoroughly combing and brushing the dog to loosen dead hair and dirt. Then step back and decide whether the dog needs to be stripped of more accumulated dead hair. Stripping means gently pulling out the dead, loose hairs by hand. A stripping knife is a tool for stripping the dog's coat, and is easier for the novice to remove the dead hairs with than hand stripping.

Before you use your stripping knives, first dull them by running the blades over an old brick. Start with the coarse knife and gently comb the blade through the coat in the direction of growth to remove the dead and loose hairs. Use a light hand, since the blade of the stripping knife may touch the skin of the dog and cause discomfort. Longer hairs are removed in small amounts with a straight pull, without bending your wrist. To protect the skin under the hair,

Use the stripping knives to remove dead hair from the dog's coat.

always pull in the direction in which the hair grows. Begin at the head and pro-
ceed to the neck and shoulders, then the back and thighs, ending with the sides.

The fine stripping knife removes the undercoat. Care must be taken not
to remove too much of the undercoat, which is the dog's jacket. A dog with
too much undercoat stripped out loses the efficiency and comfort of this
jacket.

Some terrier groomers only hand strip, gently pulling the dead and loose
hairs in the direction of their growth. If you are hand stripping, do only a little
at a time. The JRT does not enjoy long stripping sessions. Stripping is an art, so
have your dog's breeder show you how to groom your terrier.

When all the long hair has been pulled and your dog looks like he is in his
underwear, you can let him rest a bit while you trim his nails, carefully remove
unwanted hair from between his toes using the scissors, and generally check him
all over, as described in the weekly routine for a smooth-coated dog.

When this grooming procedure has been completed, mark the date on a cal-
endar and circle the date ten days from then. On the tenth day, rake out the
undercoat with the trimmer knife, which is used only for raking and never for
stripping. A trimmer knife has teeth on one side and a wooden handle. Use it
sparingly, because this tool can cut the hairs—it is only used for combing the
dog lightly between uses of the stripping knives. (Do not dull the trimmer knife

as you did the stripping knives.) This is a sharp instrument, so be very careful not to dig into the coat.

Some people prefer to use a piece of volcanic rock, found in equine supply shops and called a bot block, to maintain the coarse outer coat of the JRT. Run the volcanic rock over the dog's coat to remove the hairs that stick up. This tool is handy for grooming the legs, because grooming them may be uncomfortable for the dog with other tools and knives.

Many dogs have thick areas of coat growth over the knees that need to be thinned with thinning scissors and the volcanic rock. You can trim the hair on the back of the legs with grooming or thinning scissors, along with the tip of the tail if it has feathering or a flag of hair on it.

Now that the basic coat work is done, you will begin daily maintenance. Put the dog up on the table and, with your rubber hound glove on one hand and your horsehair glove on the other, alternately stroke the dog with each hand for five minutes. This soon becomes a favorite procedure for the JRT and, again, gives you an opportunity to examine him. After the "gloving" has been completed, selectively pluck the individual long hairs using your fingers. Gently pluck the hairs that will be sticking up. At this point, you will find that there will be a fair number of such long hairs but, as the days go by and the plucking continues, the "jacket" becomes tighter and there will be fewer and fewer hairs that stick out.

You can lightly trim the hair in the back of the legs, the tip of the tail, and around the feet.

Every week during the grooming session, rake the coat using the trimmer knife to remove excess undercoat. If this is not done, the topcoat will begin to lift and start to look like a hay field gone awry. Your JRT will appear very untidy.

The Show Coat

The coat of the Jack Russell is never sculpted; it should not be altered in such a manner as to give it an artificial, overdone appearance. Grooming should not be done to try to cover any conformation faults. This is a natural earthdog and his look should reflect that attitude. If you are showing your JRT, the judge will be looking for the dog who best suits the standard of the working terrier and who he or she would most like to take out into the field that day. Exaggerated leg furnishings and beards are not requirements of that standard. If your dog is a pet and is never shown in any conformation contest, you still will want to go over the coat weekly to keep the hairs from being shed in your house. You may use the plan above. Go over the dog at least once a week.

I like to refer to the conformation contests as the bathing suit competition. The judge is able to look at the dog to see if he is fit for the work of hunting and built for the job of earth work. Showing Jack Russell Terriers means showing of working terriers. There is not an enormous emphasis on grooming at JRTCA-sanctioned terrier trials. Dogs appear in the ring sometimes with dirt in their coats from work or missing teeth. It is not held against the dog. However, it is nice to see a well-groomed dog. A dog looking his best—fit, healthy, well constructed, and also well turned out—is a lovely package to behold.

Bathing

It is not necessary to bathe a Jack Russell Terrier unless he gets skunked, rolls in something completely objectionable, or has a serious flea problem. If a bath truly becomes necessary, be sure his ears are plugged with cotton balls and his eyes are protected from soap. Most dogs do not like baths, and the added stress of soapy eyes may make for more resistance to a bath the next time around.

The shampoo you choose should be made especially for dogs with a harsh coat. Anything that contains a conditioner will prove detrimental to the jacket. Terrier coats are, for the most part, very harsh, and they should stay that way.

Above all, be certain that all soapy residue is completely rinsed out and that the coat is thoroughly dried before the dog is allowed outdoors. If you are bathing an older animal, use a hair dryer to help dry the coat and keep the dog inside until he is completely dry, except for a brief time out to relieve himself.

How to Trim Nails

Always keep your JRT's nails well tended. If you are diligent about trimming nails, you should have no trouble maintaining a well-rounded foot—which your dog needs to move properly. Ideally, you will have the opportunity to manicure the nails from puppyhood, thereby establishing proper ground rules and conduct. Handle your puppy's feet often to get him used to being touched and held this way.

When clipping nails, it is of the utmost importance that you work in the best light possible. You should be quite able to see the quick (the bundle of nerves and blood vessels running down the center of the nail) very clearly and not clip into it. (If a nail is black, cut it back about the same amount as the clear ones, erring on the side of less rather than more.) Please do not try to cut as close as possible to the quick the first few times you trim your dog's nails. And even if you think a nail is not short enough after you have just cut it, do not clip that nail again. If you hurt the dog, it will be just that much harder to get the job done the next time. If you happen to nip the nail close enough to cause the dog discomfort, quickly apply styptic powder. Then cut the next several nails longer so the dog does not get the idea that nail clippers mean pain.

If you are in real doubt about foot care, it is best to have your veterinarian attend to it or assist you the first few times. Do be sure that the nails are trimmed, though. Nails that are too long can cause the dog to stand and move incorrectly and can harm his feet.

Work in the best light possible when trimming nails to avoid cutting off too much and hurting your dog.

Dealing with Parasites

Jack Russells are working dogs, and that means they will be running through fields and brush and other places where they can pick up very nasty parasites. As I mentioned at the beginning of this chapter, regular grooming sessions are a good way to check your dog for fleas and ticks. Use a metal flea comb to comb through every inch of the dog's body. These nasty parasites are a continuous and potentially serious, even deadly, problem for your dog. Preventing fleas and ticks is better than trying to remove them when they have taken up residence on your dog or in your home.

Ticks

Various species of ticks may attach themselves to your dog. In addition to Lyme disease, ticks can also carry such ailments as Rocky Mountain spotted fever and canine ehrlichiosis. Prompt removal of ticks will help prevent the transmission of these diseases.

The most common areas where you will find ticks are the ears, neck and head, and between the toes. If you find only a few ticks on your dog, the easiest thing to do is remove them as described in the box on page 69.

During regular grooming sessions, be sure to use the fine-tooth comb to check your dog for parasites.

How to Get Rid of a Tick

During tick season (which, depending on where you live, can be spring, summer, and/or fall), examine your dog every day for ticks. Pay particular attention to your dog's neck, behind the ears, the armpits, and the groin.

When you find a tick, use a cotton ball or swab to dab it with a bit of alcohol. Wait a few minutes, then use a pair of tweezers to grasp the tick as close as possible to the dog's skin and pull it out using firm, steady pressure. Check to make sure you get the whole tick (mouth parts left in your dog's skin can cause an infection), then dab the wound with a little hydrogen peroxide and some antibiotic ointment. Watch for signs of inflammation.

Ticks carry very serious diseases that are transmittable to humans, so dispose of the tick safely. *Never* crush it between your fingers. Don't flush it down the toilet either, because the tick will survive the trip and infect another animal. Instead, use the tweezers to place the tick in a tight-sealing jar or plastic dish with a little alcohol, put on the lid and dispose of the container in an outdoor garbage can. Wash the tweezers thoroughly with hot water and alcohol.

Sarcoptic Mange

This condition is caused by a microscopic arachnid called a mite. Jack Russells love to poke around in holes they discover, and if the last resident of that hole carried mange mites, the JRT may pick them up. Mange appears in many areas of the country and is especially hard on red foxes, which are often seen missing large patches of their red coat and proud brush (tail).

Mange frequently shows up first on the face, ears, belly, or thighs of the dog, and then spreads with itchy patches of missing hair and scabbed areas of skin. The mite feeds and reproduces on the dog, and treatment by a veterinarian is required.

Making Your Environment Flea Free

If there are fleas on your dog, there are fleas in your home, yard, and car, even if you can't see them. You must break the lifecycle of the fleas to remove them. All these steps will have to take place to break the cycle.

In your home:

- Wash whatever is washable (the dog bed, sheets, blankets, pillow covers, slipcovers, curtains, etc.).
- Vacuum everything else in your home—furniture, floors, rugs, everything. Pay special attention to the folds and crevices in upholstery, cracks between floorboards, and the spaces between the floor and the baseboards. Flea larvae are sensitive to sunlight, so inside the house they prefer deep carpet, bedding, and cracks and crevices.
- When you're done, throw the vacuum cleaner bag away—in an outside garbage can.
- Use a nontoxic flea-killing powder, such as Flea Busters or Zodiac FleaTrol, to treat your carpets (but remember, it does not control fleas elsewhere in the house). The powder stays deep in the carpet and kills fleas (using a form of boric acid) for up to a year.
- If you have a particularly serious flea problem, consider using a fogger or long-lasting spray to kill any adult and larval fleas, or having a professional exterminator treat your home.

If your dog has mange mites, you may find that you, too, are itching. Fortunately, though, the mites cannot complete their life cycle on humans and will not last long there (provided the dog has been successfully treated).

Fleas

These pests are a long-standing annoyance to dogs and owners. Flea "dirt" (digested dog blood) can be seen as dark specks in the dog's coat. If the "dirt" is moistened, it becomes a rusty red color, distinguishing it from soil. White specks that you may find on your dog are flea eggs.

The saliva of the flea is very irritating, and dogs who are allergic to the saliva will break out in a rash, called flea allergy dermatitis. The itching can become so

In your car:

- Take out the floor mats and hose them down with a strong stream of water, then hang them up to dry in the sun.
- Wash any towels, blankets, or other bedding you regularly keep in the car.
- Thoroughly vacuum the entire interior of your car, paying special attention to the seams between the bottom and back of the seats.
- When you're done, throw the vacuum cleaner bag away—in an outside garbage can.

In your yard:

- Flea larvae prefer shaded areas that have plenty of organic material and moisture, so rake the yard thoroughly and bag all the debris in tightly sealed bags.
- Spray your yard with an insecticide that has residual activity for at least thirty days. Insecticides that use a form of boric acid are nontoxic. Some newer products contain an insect growth regulator (such as fenoxycarb) and need to be applied only once or twice a year.
- For an especially difficult flea problem, consider having an exterminator treat your yard.
- Keep your yard free of piles of leaves, weeds, and other organic debris. Be especially careful in shady, moist areas, such as under bushes.

severe that, because of constant scratching and biting, hair is lost in affected areas, primarily the base of the tail, inner thighs, and backs of the rear legs.

Fleas flourish in a warm, humid environment. Having fallen off the dog and found a cozy place to incubate, it takes only a few days for the eggs to hatch into larvae. The larvae spin a cocoon, go into a pupal stage and, in good conditions, adult fleas will emerge in two or three weeks—though the pupal stage can also last up to several months.

After hatching, the fleas go looking for food. They are hardy critters, and if they can't find any food right away, they can go without for many months. This is why it is important to rid your home as well as your dog of these parasites. As soon as your JRT walks by and provides a tasty meal for a flea, the life cycle begins once again. One female flea can lay thousands of eggs in her lifetime.

New Products in the Fight Against Fleas

At one time, battling fleas meant exposing your dog and yourself to toxic dips, sprays, powders, and collars. But today there are flea preventives that work very well and are safe for your dog, you, and the environment. The two most common types are insect growth regulators (IGRs), which stop the immature flea from developing or maturing, and adult flea killers. To deal with an active infestation, experts usually recommend a product that has both.

You may want to consider using one of the many new flea prevention medications to prevent fleas and ticks on your dog. This is a very personal decision that requires a conference with your veterinarian.

These next-generation flea fighters generally come in one of two forms:

- **Topical treatments or spot-ons.** These products are applied to the skin, usually between the shoulder blades. The product is absorbed through the skin into the dog's system. Among the most widely available spot-ons are Advantage (kills adult fleas and larvae), Revolution (kills adult fleas), Frontline Plus (kills adult fleas and larvae, plus an IGR), K-9 Advantix (kills adult fleas and larvae), and BioSpot (kills adult fleas and larvae, plus an IGR).
- **Systemic products.** This is a pill your dog swallows that transmits a chemical throughout the dog's bloodstream. When a flea bites the dog, it picks up this chemical, which then prevents the flea's eggs from developing. Among the most widely available systemic products are Program (kills larvae only, plus an IGR) and Capstar (kills adult fleas).

Make sure you read all the labels and apply the products exactly as recommended, and that you check to make sure they are safe for puppies.

How to Control Fleas

The most effective means of flea control involves breaking the lifecycle. If you have a serious infestation, bathe your dog with a flea shampoo and thoroughly clean your home and environment, as described in the box on pages 70 and 71.

Many people are concerned about using chemicals on their dogs and in their homes or kennel areas. New flea control products (see the box on page 72) have greatly reduced this concern. Still, these are chemicals and the flea must bite the dog to get a fatal dose.

You may want to consider the alternative of food-quality diatomaceous earth, which is dusted on the dog and his bedding. Diatomaceous earth is the fossilized remains of marine organisms with microscopic sharp edges that cause the immature stages of the flea to dehydrate. Food-quality diatomaceous earth is harmless to humans and animals. Unfortunately, it will not kill adult fleas.

A very effective way to safely keep fleas in check is to comb your dog out of doors every day, or almost every day, during flea season. All you will need is a fine flea comb and a glass of water into which you have mixed a few drops of mild liquid soap. When the comb picks up fleas, quickly dip it into the soapy water and remove the fleas from the comb. (The soap coats the flea and kills it.) Keep the glass close to you. If it is too far away, those critters may have time to jump off the comb. The jumping ability of fleas is the equivalent of a person jumping the as high as the Empire State Building. They are the super athletes of the pest world.

If you gently handle your dog's feet, ears, eyes, and teeth regularly when she is a puppy, she will be cooperative during grooming sessions as an adult.

Chapter 8

Keeping Your Jack Russell Terrier Healthy

Having explored the intelligence and charm and, perhaps, the not so charming attributes of the Jack Russell Terrier, it is worth noting here that the Jack Russell seems to have fewer inherited problems than many other dog breeds. Most Jack Russells can live long, healthy, happy lives when they are provided with safe surroundings and the exercise and close companionship they crave and demand.

Preventive Care

Most health problems are preventable. Vaccinations, a yearly health examination by your dog's veterinarian, good nutrition, adequate daily exercise, and loving companionship are the most important things you can provide for your dog to keep her healthy, both mentally and physically.

As soon as possible after you bring home your puppy or adult dog, you should take her to your veterinarian for a physical examination, any vaccinations that are due, a parasite check, and, if necessary, worming. In addition to the pedigree and stud certificate, the breeder or previous owner should have provided you with the dog's health records, current through the date of purchase.

Be sure to discuss your dog's vaccination schedule with your veterinarian. Not all dogs need all vaccines, and decisions must be made (see the box on page 78). Some dog owners, not wanting to over-vaccinate their dogs with routine injections, have blood tests called titers done once a year to check their dog's immunity levels.

Make your trip to the veterinarian a pleasant one. You should not act nervous or make a fuss over the trip or any procedure, as your Jack Russell will be sure to pick up on your feelings. Your dog's introduction to his doctor should be very matter-of-fact.

Another important component of preventive care is making sure all the working parts of your working terrier are in good order. Keeping eyes, ears, and teeth clean and healthy is important for maintaining a happy, healthy pet.

Ears

The ears on the Jack Russell fold over, which, in theory, is to help keep dirt out of the inner ear when the dogs are below ground. If you see your dog shaking her head or scratching her ears, or if there is an unpleasant odor, dirt might be embedded in the ear, there may be an infection, or ear mites could be present. Your veterinarian can give you a diagnosis.

If the problem is ear mites, the vet will prescribe drops to eliminate them. Mites are highly contagious and all pets in the home should be checked and treated.

Inspect your dog's ears weekly to keep ahead of any problems that may arise. You may want to use a liquid ear cleansing product. Clean the ears with a cotton swab, but never go farther into the ear canal than you can see.

Inspect and clean your dog's ears weekly.

Eyes

Eye care is important, and eyes should be checked every week, or after the dog has been working below ground. When a Jack Russell follows her nose and instincts, she will enter an earthen den and probably end up with dirt or particles of sand in her eyes. If this foreign matter is not removed, the corneas may be scratched.

Even nonworking dogs will often have foreign matter in their eyes. You can wash out the eyes with lukewarm water or a special eye-cleaning preparation. Pull the lids back to make sure there is no dirt hiding in the corners of the eye.

Never use medication in the dog's eyes that has not been prescribed by your veterinarian.

Teeth

Dental care is important to your dog's overall health, and brushing and scaling her teeth help promote good dental hygiene. Tartar deposits build up quickly, particularly on the back upper molars and the canines, leading to gum disease. Puppies can be trained to accept dental care if the process is done frequently. Keep the sessions upbeat and short.

There are toothbrushes designed especially for dogs, and gauze wrapped around your finger also works. Because a dog cannot spit, she will swallow the toothpaste, so please be sure to use a formulation made especially for dogs. Tooth scalers can be obtained from a canine products catalog, where you can also buy the toothbrushes and toothpaste.

Regular tooth brushing is as important for your dog as it is for you.

Have your dog's teeth checked at least once a year by the veterinarian. It may sometimes be necessary for the vet to clean your dog's teeth more thoroughly, particularly if your dog is older. Your veterinarian will sedate your dog for this procedure. Advances in canine anesthesia make this procedure much safer now than in the past.

Neglected teeth may lead to periodontal disease. The bacteria can enter the bloodstream and are associated with other diseases of the heart, liver, and kidneys. Watch for red or bleeding gums. Bad breath is another major indication that the dog needs to visit the vet for treatment.

Anal Glands

Anal glands provide lubrication for the passing of stools and also function as scent glands. The sacs that produce these secretions are located on either side and slightly down from the anus. They normally empty when the dog defecates, but may have a tendency to fill or even become blocked in some dogs, and so should be checked from time to time.

When a dog scoots along the ground, it may be a sign of worms or it could mean the anal sacs are plugged and the dog is trying to empty them. They are irritating and can make the dog uncomfortable. And, left untreated, a nasty infection can develop.

Expressing the sacs can easily be done by any JRT owner. Using a soft cloth or tissue, take the skin of the anus and pull it outward with a gentle, twisting motion. This gentle action encourages the sacs to empty. Be warned that the contents of the anal glands possess a very powerful disagreeable odor. You will not want to get it on you or your clothing.

If you see any blood or pus in the secretions, take your dog to the veterinarian.

Internal Parasites

When you first get your dog or puppy and take her for her first visit to your veterinarian, be sure to bring along the health records the breeder or previous owner gave to you. These records should reflect not only the vaccinations your dog has received, but also a schedule of dewormings. Also bring with you a fresh stool sample for analysis. The vet can quickly diagnose what, if any, types of worms your dog is harboring, so treatment can begin right away.

Please do not think that over-the-counter remedies for parasites will work properly. Only your dog's veterinarian is qualified to diagnose and treat parasitic infestations. Medicating your dog yourself can cause you to lose precious time your vet may need to help your dog or puppy, or even save her life. Improper use of worming medications can be toxic if given incorrectly. Always consult with your veterinarian regarding control of internal parasites.

The best way of controlling internal parasites is cleanliness. Always keep feces picked up and keep your dog free of fleas. Maintain a clean and dry environment to discourage the further development of eggs and larvae and disinfect dog areas. A solution of three cups of bleach to one gallon of water is a good disinfectant to use.

Roundworms

If your puppy's dam has ever had roundworms (and it is quite likely that she has), her pups probably will be born with roundworms. Some larvae encyst in the mother's tissue and, in the late stages of pregnancy, the dormant larvae are released and carried to the unborn puppies. They are also passed on through breast milk. This is why it is always advisable to deworm a female before she is bred—although doing so will not rid her of the encysted larvae. For this reason, puppies must be dewormed by the time they are two or three weeks of age.

Vaccines

What vaccines dogs need and how often they need them has been a subject of controversy for several years. Researchers, health care professionals, vaccine manufacturers, and dog owners do not always agree on which vaccines each dog needs or how often booster shots must be given.

In 2003, the American Animal Hospital Association released vaccination guidelines and recommendations that have helped dog owners and veterinarians sort through much of the controversy and conflicting information. The guidelines designate four vaccines as core, or essential, because of the serious nature of the diseases and their widespread distribution. These are canine distemper virus, canine parvovirus, canine adenovirus-2, and rabies. The general recommendations for their use (except rabies, for which you must follow local laws) are:

- Vaccinate puppies at 6–8 weeks, 9–11 weeks, and 12–14 weeks.
- Give a booster shot when the dog is 1 year old.

Roundworms will be passed in the feces. The treatment should be repeated at least once more about two weeks later. A third, or even fourth, course of treatment may be necessary if worms are found after the previous treatment. The usual medication used to treat roundworms in puppies is very safe. Roundworms are not much of a problem in adults, but puppies can die from a heavy infestation.

Hookworms

The same medication used to treat roundworms is also very effective against hookworms. It is uncommon for a pup to be born with hookworms, but these parasites can be acquired through the mother's milk during the first two or three weeks of life. Left unchecked, an affected puppy can quickly die.

- Give a subsequent booster shot every three years, unless there are risk factors that make it necessary to vaccinate more or less often.

Noncore vaccines should only be considered for those dogs who risk exposure to a particular disease because of geographic area, lifestyle, frequency of travel, or other issues. They include vaccines against distemper-measles virus, canine parainfluenza virus, leptospirosis, Bordetella bronchiseptica, and Borrelia burgdorferi (Lyme disease).

Vaccines that are not generally recommended because the disease poses little risk to dogs or is easily treatable, or the vaccine has not been proven to be effective, are those against Giardia, canine coronavirus, and canine adenovirus-1.

Often, combination injections are given to puppies, with one shot containing several core and noncore vaccines. Your veterinarian may be reluctant to use separate shots that do not include the noncore vaccines, because they must be specially ordered. If you are concerned about these noncore vaccines, talk to your vet.

Whipworms

These are a third type of internal parasite to contend with. Because the female whipworm lays fewer eggs than most other worms, it can be harder to detect their presence. When whipworms are found, a relatively long course of treatment is required to eliminate them.

Tapeworms

Perhaps the most familiar internal parasite for dog owners is the tapeworm. There are different kinds of tapeworms, but the most common is the one transmitted by fleas. (The flea ingests tapeworm eggs when it bites an infected animal and your dog then swallows the flea.) Another type of tapeworm is acquired by

Puppies can acquire roundworms and hookworms from their mother.

eating animal parts, including mice. The head of the worm attaches to the wall of the gut; the body is made up of segments that contain the eggs. By the time you see segments in the feces or in the dog's hair around the anus (they look like grains of rice), there is probably a fairly heavy infestation. See your veterinarian immediately for treatment.

Heartworms

Heartworms are very serious and difficult to treat, but can be prevented from infecting your dog. After a bite from an infected mosquito, larvae work their way into the dog and eventually develop into small adult worms. The worms then enter the bloodstream and travel to the heart, where they mature. The female gives birth to thousands of live young, called microfilaria, which move into the bloodstream and wait for their host (the mosquito) to come along to help them develop into larvae ready to infect another dog.

Dozens of heartworms, up to twelve inches long, have been found in the heart of just one dog. There may be no symptoms of infestation for several years, and even then the early symptoms may be misinterpreted. Left untreated, a heartworm infestation can be fatal.

Prevention is vital for the safety of your dog. Blood is drawn and tested to ensure that the dog is free from infection. If he is, your veterinarian will prescribe a heartworm preventive to be given in daily or monthly doses. Depending upon where you live, you may have to administer the drug year-round. In colder areas, where mosquitoes retire for the winter, you may be able to stop the preventing medication for a few months. Your veterinarian will tell you what procedure must be followed.

The devastation caused to a dog's heart and lungs by heartworms is unimaginable and unnecessary. Responsible pet owners will not hesitate to initiate a regimen of prevention for the life of their pets.

Protozoans

Other, different types of parasites may trouble your dog. Known as protozoans, they are one-celled animals, invisible to the naked eye, that invade the intestinal tract. Again, unsanitary, overcrowded conditions are the usual cause. The primary symptom is diarrhea, which may affect puppies more quickly and seriously than adults. Your veterinarian must be consulted; diagnosis can be confirmed through fecal tests.

JRTs have fewer inherited problems than many breeds, but, like all dogs, they can still be born with health issues.

Problems Seen in the Jack Russell

As I have already mentioned, Jack Russells seem to have fewer inherited problems than many other dog breeds. Responsible breeders work hard to identify genetic problems in their dogs, and dogs with known defects should not be bred. However, as in all dogs, some genetic problems have been found in Jack Russells.

Luxating Patella

A luxating patella is a slipped kneecap. The kneecap (patella) tends to pop out of the joint because the groove in the thighbone (femur) in which it sits is too shallow. When the patella becomes dislocated, there may be pain and difficulty straightening the knee. The luxation may be permanent or it may be intermittent, with the kneecap popping in and out of position. The dog may move in a normal manner one minute and be lame the next.

This condition can lead to the premature development of arthritis and restricted, painful movement. This is the last thing you want an eager, active dog like the Jack Russell to go through. If the condition becomes painful, corrective surgery is the preferred treatment, and patients usually recover fully.

Legg-Perthes Disease

Legg-Perthes disease is seen in many breeds of small dogs. It is caused by a destruction of the blood supply to the ball part of the ball-and-socket hip joint, which causes the bone tissue to die. Pain and stiffness, leading to arthritis, is the result. Mild cases can be managed with medication, but for serious cases surgery is the best option.

Deafness

Deafness shows up more often in white-coated animals, and therefore may be linked genetically to coat color. The dog may be totally deaf (bilateral) or deaf in only one ear (unilateral). Unilateral deafness is more difficult to detect, as the dog quickly learns to compensate for her loss. A BAER (brainstem auditory evoked response) test is used to detect deafness; it measures the brain's response to sound.

It takes a very dedicated owner with very special abilities to provide for the protection and safety of a totally deaf Jack Russell. Some deaf dogs do well living with hearing dogs, or with deaf people who have taught the dog sign language. But there are also incidents of biting, which have occurred as a result of an exaggerated startle response from a deaf dog.

A bilaterally (both ears) or unilaterally deaf dog must not be bred. It is strongly suggested that all breeding stock be BAER tested before they are bred. The test is not difficult or painful for the dog.

Hernia

A hernia is a protrusion of an organ or tissue through the abdominal wall. Umbilical (in the navel area) and inguinal (in the groin) hernias are the types most commonly seen in dogs. The blood supply to the protrusion may eventually be cut off, causing complications. Mild hernias in puppies sometimes close on their own. They must be watched closely, and, if necessary, surgically repaired. A dog born with a hernia should not be bred.

Deafness may be genetically linked to the white coat color. Responsible breeders screen their dogs before they are bred.

Lens Luxation

Lens luxation, a dislocation of the lens of the eye, usually appears during a dog's middle age. It is an inherited disease of the tissues that hold the lens in place. Both eyes are usually affected and secondary glaucoma may result.

Surgery is needed to remove the affected lens or lenses. Vision after surgery will be reduced but still present. This treatment, while not perfect, is certainly preferable to blindness—secondary glaucoma will gradually destroy vision altogether.

High Toes

High toes have been seen on Jack Russells. This involves a toe that is set high on the foot, usually on the outside. It occurs mainly on the front feet but has been found on back feet also. This defect may appear in particular bloodlines and is being studied.

Von Willebrand's Disease

Von Willebrand's disease (vWD) is the most common inherited bleeding disorder in dogs. Both males and females carry it, and both sexes can be affected.

Bleeding in affected individuals is caused by a deficiency or dysfunction of the von Willebrand factor (vWF) protein, normally found in plasma and critical in the control of bleeding. A dog may be a carrier but not be affected and not show any symptoms. Affected dogs may show symptoms such as spontaneous bleeding from mucous membrane linings of the nose or mouth, or prolonged bleeding from sites of trauma or surgery, or even after clipping a nail too short.

In addition to having been found in more than fifty breeds of dogs, von Willebrand's disease has been seen in mixed-breed dogs, cats, horses, pigs, and human beings. It is not common in Jack Russells, but it has been found.

There is no treatment for controlling von Willebrand's disease, although a drug can be administered to increase clotting during a crisis. Since it is known to be hereditary, any dog with a history of this disease in his background should be tested. Dogs should also be tested for it prior to breeding.

First-Aid Situations

Wildlife Encounters

The call of the wild is irresistible to Jack Russells. On any given day, while walking in the woods your Jack Russell may find himself face to face with some form of wildlife. A groundhog bite heals quickly and rarely infects, but an encounter

This dog has treed a squirrel. Wildlife encounters can hold many dangers for your JRT.

with a raccoon is a more serious matter. Raccoons may carry rabies or coonhound paralysis, and they have been known to drown even large dogs if they are near a body of water. Raccoons who are seen during daylight hours are probably sick. They should be avoided at all costs.

Skunks are also to be avoided, and not just for the obvious reason. Along with raccoons, skunks often carry rabies. If a skunk sprays a Jack Russell in close quarters (such as in a hole), the dog is at risk of dying. The spraying affects lung function and it is vital to get the dog to a veterinarian immediately for oxygen and additional treatment. If the

How to Make a Canine First-Aid Kit

If your dog hurts herself, even a minor cut, it can be very upsetting for both of you. Having a first-aid kit handy will help you to help her, calmly and efficiently. What should be in your canine first-aid kit?

- Activated charcoal
- Antibiotic ointment
- Antiseptic and antibacterial cleansing wipes
- Benadryl
- Cotton-tipped applicators
- Disposable razor
- Elastic wrap bandages
- Extra leash and collar
- First-aid tape of various widths
- Gauze bandage roll
- Gauze pads of different sizes, including eye pads
- Hydrogen peroxide
- Instant cold compress
- Ipecac syrup
- Kaopectate tablets or liquid
- Latex gloves
- Lubricating jelly
- Milk of magnesia
- Mineral oil
- Muzzle
- Nail clippers
- Pen, pencil, and paper for notes and directions
- Pepto-Bismol
- Round-ended scissors and pointy scissors
- Safety pins
- Sterile saline eyewash
- Thermometer (rectal)
- Tweezers

spraying is above ground, there are commercial products that are effective to reduce the odor. Also, bathing the dog in tomato juice is still accepted as being quite effective.

Porcupine quills must be removed quickly and completely by a veterinarian. The quills are very painful and will continue to work themselves deeper and deeper into the dog. There are cases where porcupine quills have killed Jack Russells. Treatment must not be delayed.

Insect Stings

Insect stings are annoying, cause swelling, and may bring on allergic reactions in some dogs. Multiple stings may cause shock. Your veterinarian will instruct you on the treatment required for insect stings, and perhaps suggest an antihistamine to control swelling. Watch the site for any signs of infection.

Vomiting

Vomiting should not be of any great concern if it does not persist. If your JRT has eaten something that has upset her stomach and she vomits, just keep a close eye on her. If she vomits three times or more and seems withdrawn or lethargic, call your veterinarian immediately, whether or not any other symptoms are present.

Choking

Choking can be a life-threatening condition. Puppies, who are curious by nature, are always picking up all sorts of objects and are the most susceptible to choking on so many of the things that catch their eye. You may be able to reach into the dog's throat and dislodge the object, or you may have to perform the canine Heimlich maneuver. Lay the dog on her side and, with your palms just behind the last rib, give four quick thrusts. Check the mouth for the object and repeat the maneuver if necessary.

Some objects have been known to become dislodged by holding the dog upside down. In a last-ditch effort to save his life, I had to perform a tracheotomy on one of my Jack Russells in order to open an air passage. He had fallen unconscious and his heart had stopped beating. With that emergency action, mouth-to-muzzle resuscitation, and gentle chest compression, the dog survived. He had been choking on a piece of rawhide.

Poisons

Poisons and toxins that can be dangerous for your Jack Russell are all over: house, garden, garage, everywhere. In your house may be such plants as dieffenbachia, philodendron, asparagus fern, ivy, and poinsettia. Also dangerous are all the pesticides, cleaning supplies, and medicines that must be closely guarded. In the garden are acorns, lily of the valley, wisteria, daffodils, morning glory, holly, rhubarb, and tomato vine, among others.

ASPCA Animal Poison Control Center

The ASPCA Animal Poison Control Center has a staff of licensed veterinarians and board-certified toxicologists available 24 hours a day, 365 days a year. The number to call is (888) 426-4435. You will be charged a consultation fee of $50 per case, charged to most major credit cards. There is no charge for follow-up calls in critical cases. At your request, they will also contact your veterinarian. Specific treatment and information can be provided via fax. Put the number in large, legible print with your other emergency telephone numbers. Be prepared to give your name, address, and phone number; what your dog has gotten into (the amount and how long ago); your dog's breed, age, sex, and weight; and what signs and symptoms the dog is showing. You can log onto www.aspca.org and click on "Animal Poison Control Center" for more information, including a list of toxic and nontoxic plants.

And in the garage are any number of dangerous toxins, including the very common, sweet-tasting antifreeze (also a danger to children). Even a small amount carelessly left on the garage floor may kill.

And then there is chocolate. Some dogs love chocolate. But a lethal dose consists of only one ounce of milk chocolate or one-third ounce of dark chocolate per pound of dog.

Symptoms of poisoning can range from obvious residue around your dog's mouth, to rashes on the skin or around the mouth, to vomiting and diarrhea, to hallucinations and convulsions, among others.

If you suspect that your dog has been poisoned, immediate action is necessary. First, try to identify the poison, then call your veterinarian. If chemicals are involved, read the label and have it handy when you talk to your vet, or call ASPCA Animal Poison Control (see the box above) for information on the chemical if the label is not informative.

If your vet is not available, ASPCA Animal Poison Control also can instruct you on the proper procedures to follow. Depending on the substance ingested, the length of time it has been in your dog's system, and the dog's condition, you may be

These dogs are brave sometimes to the point of recklessness. It's up to you to protect your dog from the dangers in her environment.

instructed either to induce vomiting with ipecac syrup or hydrogen peroxide, or to give activated charcoal to delay or prevent absorption. Those items are important to have on hand, as well as other aids such as milk of magnesia and mineral oil.

Heat Stroke

Heat stroke, also known as hyperthermia, occurs when the dog's internal temperature is higher than 104 degrees. (A dog's normal temperature is between 100 and 102 degrees.) Dogs cannot tolerate heat as well as humans can. They must pant to cool their bodies and the only place they are able to sweat is through their foot pads. Heavy exertion, especially in hot weather, can therefore be problematic.

Since Jack Russells often do not know when to stop and rest to cool off, they may overdo it and show signs of hyperthermia. Symptoms include extreme weakness or panting, rapid breathing, vomiting, and fainting. The dog may also have an elevated heart rate.

> **CAUTION**
>
> For the safety of your JRT, temperature extremes, hot or cold, are to be avoided. Be sure the dog has shade and other appropriate shelter when she is outdoors, as well as a good supply of fresh, cool water always available. In winter, guard against the dog getting frostbitten.

In mild cases, moving the dog to an air-conditioned room may solve the problem. Apply cool compresses to the abdomen and groin and offer sips of cool water. For more serious cases, cool the dog gradually in water. Do not try to bring down the temperature too rapidly. In all cases, call your veterinarian immediately. Serious hyperthermia can lead to coma and death.

Never, ever leave your dog in the car in warm weather—not even for a few minutes, even if the windows are open. It is far better to leave the dog at home, no matter how much she loves to travel with you, if there is even a chance that you will have to leave her alone in the vehicle. Just a short stop at the store may put you at the end of a very long line at the checkout, and temperatures in parked cars can reach life-threatening levels very, very quickly.

Shock

Shock is a danger to Jack Russells who may have exerted themselves greatly and have been without water for a period of time. Shock may also result from accident, injury, or blood loss. The dog will be weak and have pale gums, take shallow breaths, and have a rapid, weak pulse. Her eyes will have a glazed look and her body temperature will be low.

Any dog in shock must be kept warm. Immediately wrap the dog in a blanket or your own jacket and get her to a veterinarian as soon as possible.

Dehydration

Dehydration is a danger in both hot and cold weather. Always remember to bring water with you for you and your JRT when hiking and enjoying other outdoor activities together.

In an emergency, your dog will rely on you.

Bleeding

Bleeding requires you to remain calm so you can help your dog. Try not to excite the dog; talk to her soothingly to help her keep still. Apply gentle pressure on the wound with your hand or fingers, using a clean cloth if one is available. Dress the wound with a bandage but do not pull it too tightly. You may apply an ice pack to keep the area cold in order to slow the bleeding. Get to a veterinarian, where the wound can be cleaned and sutured, if necessary.

Dehydration is always a danger for such an active breed. Always bring water with you when you take your JRT out for any activity. (These dogs are racing at a JRTCA field trial.)

Fractures

A dog with a fracture may hold her injured leg off the ground or cry in pain. If a bone is broken, you will need to get your JRT to the veterinarian immediately. Slip the dog onto a piece of plywood or other sturdy surface to be transported. Try to keep the injured limb immobile. It's good if someone can help you calm the dog and keep her still.

If there is no fracture, it is possible the dog picked up a thorn or other object that has punctured or become imbedded in her pad or the soft tissue between the toes.

Loss of Appetite

If your dog refuses to eat for more than a day or two, or has diarrhea or a cough, call the veterinarian. These could be symptoms of a number of ailments. (If the dog has diarrhea, remove all food but be sure fresh, clean water is available.)

Jack Russells are tough little dogs and recover quickly from almost any problem, but they do have a tendency to eat icky things, bringing on any number of consequences or, surprisingly, no consequences at all. My favorite true JRTs-eat-icky-things story happened one day when a neighbor's dog jumped up into a bush, caught a sparrow, and consumed it in one giant swallow. His concerned owners called their veterinarian and asked what they should do. Knowing the breed well, the doctor mused for a moment and replied, "May I suggest an orange sauce?"

Muzzles

Even the sweetest dog in the world may try to bite you out of instinct if you handle her when she is injured or in pain. Get a secure, comfortable muzzle and practice putting it on the dog for successively longer periods, up to a few minutes at a time. Try to make this fun, be gentle, and reward her for calmly accepting the restraint. If your dog is at least familiar with a muzzle ahead of time, she may be spared the added anxiety of having to cope with a strange new device when she has been hurt.

If you race your Jack Russell at a terrier trial, she will be very familiar with wearing a muzzle without any disagreement. Some associate the muzzle with the fun of racing.

If an emergency arises and you do not have a muzzle, you can make one from a strip of soft cloth, a necktie, or even a stocking. Keep the dog calm and speak to her in a reassuring tone of voice. Holding one end of the cloth in each hand, make a loop, and close it with a half-knot. Slip the loop around the Jack Russell's muzzle, with the half-knot on top, and tighten it. Make a second loop around the muzzle and tighten it

The sooner you take your dog to the vet when you suspect an illness, the quicker she will recover.

When to Call the Veterinarian

Go to the vet right away or take your dog to an emergency veterinary clinic if:

- Your dog is choking.
- Your dog is having trouble breathing.
- Your dog has been injured and you cannot stop the bleeding within a few minutes.
- Your dog has been stung or bitten by an insect and the site is swelling.
- Your dog has been bitten by a snake.
- Your dog has been bitten by another animal (including a dog) and shows any swelling or bleeding.
- Your dog has touched, licked, or in any way been exposed to a poison.
- Your dog has been burned by either heat or caustic chemicals.
- Your dog has been hit by a car.
- Your dog has any obvious broken bones or cannot put any weight on one of her limbs.
- Your dog has a seizure.

Make an appointment to see the vet as soon as possible if:

- Your dog has been bitten by a cat, another dog, or a wild animal.
- Your dog has been injured and is still limping an hour later.

with a half-knot underneath. Bring the ends of the cloth around the back of the neck and tie them together securely.

Dogfights

Dogfights are common among Jack Russells. Not only will they fight among themselves, but they will often try to get it on with the biggest dog in the neighborhood, facing the danger that they will be shaken to death by a very annoyed animal many times their size. Puncture wounds from dogfights have a tendency to become infected, as well.

- Your dog has unexplained swelling or redness.
- Your dog's appetite changes.
- Your dog vomits repeatedly and can't seem to keep food down, or drools excessively while eating.
- You see any changes in your dog's urination or defecation (pain during elimination, change in regular habits, blood in urine or stool, diarrhea, foul-smelling stool).
- Your dog scoots her rear end on the floor.
- Your dog's energy level, attitude, or behavior changes for no apparent reason.
- Your dog has crusty or cloudy eyes, or excessive tearing or discharge.
- Your dog's nose is dry or chapped, hot, crusty, or runny.
- Your dog's ears smell foul, have a dark discharge, or seem excessively waxy.
- Your dog's gums are inflamed or bleeding, her teeth look brown, or her breath is foul.
- Your dog's skin is red, flaky, itchy, or inflamed, or she keeps chewing at certain spots.
- Your dog's coat is dull, dry, brittle, or bare in spots.
- Your dog's paws are red, swollen, tender, cracked, or the nails are split or too long.
- Your dog is panting excessively, wheezing, unable to catch her breath, breathing heavily or sounds strange when she breathes.

Among themselves, same-sex fights are the most common and fights between females have a history of being the most heated. It is not at all uncommon to have to place one of the offending scrappers in another household.

Prevention is the best cure. Keep your Jack Russell confined in a securely fenced yard, or leashed when you are walking in public places. Keep no more than two Jack Russells together, preferably spayed and neutered animals of the opposite sex.

If two dogs begin to square off, a distraction quickly created may end the episode. Throwing water on fighting dogs or sharply snapping a hound crop can sometimes end a confrontation if it has just begun. If the dogs are really into it and have a secure hold on each other, never try to pull them apart; you will cause more

Some JRTs will be best buddies. Others cannot tolerate the company of other dogs.

damage to the dogs and risk getting bitten by accident when the two dogs are try-ing to make contact with each other and get you instead. To break up a fight, it is necessary to securely hold both dogs on the ground or floor until one lets go, at which time you have to move fast to get them locked away from each other!

Once a serious fight has occurred between two individual dogs, it is likely that the animosity will continue and that they never will be able to be together again. Each one seems to hold a grudge against the other. Even a series of appar-ently minor scraps seem to escalate in seriousness with each successive alterca-tion. Permanently separate the offending dogs and avoid the possibility of serious injury or worse down the line.

Be aware that there is a difference between the rough-and-tumble, seemingly angry play between two JRTs and a real fight. You will clearly recognize that dif-ference if you ever have the misfortune of being present when two JRTs decide to take each other on. It is not pretty and it is not fun.

Spaying and Neutering

Neutering or spaying is the kindest thing you can do for your dog. Life with a dog is much easier for you, too, if you do not have to be concerned with the problems associated with the female's heat cycles or the male's compulsion to

Why Spay and Neuter?

Breeding dogs is a serious undertaking that should only be part of a well-planned breeding program. Why? Because dogs pass on their physical and behavioral problems to their offspring. Even healthy, well-behaved dogs can pass on problems in their genes.

Is your dog so sweet that you'd like to have a litter of puppies just like her? If you breed her to another dog, the pups will not have the same genetic heritage she has. Breeding her *parents* again will increase the odds of a similar pup, but even then, the puppies in the second litter could inherit different genes. In fact, *there is no way to breed a dog to be just like another dog.*

Meanwhile, thousands and thousands of dogs are killed in animal shelters every year simply because they have no homes. Casual breeding is a big contributor to this problem.

If you don't plan to breed your dog, is it still a good idea to spay her or neuter him? Yes!

When you spay your female:

- You avoid her heat cycles, during which she discharges blood and scent.
- It greatly reduces the risk of mammary cancer and eliminates the risk of pyometra (an often fatal infection of the uterus) and uterine cancer.
- It prevents unwanted pregnancies.
- It reduces dominance behaviors and aggression.

When you neuter your male:

- It curbs the desire to roam and to fight with other males.
- It greatly reduces the risk of prostate cancer and eliminates the risk of testicular cancer.
- It helps reduce leg lifting and mounting behavior.
- It reduces dominance behaviors and aggression.

seek a female in season. You won't have the surprise of puppies that you had not planned for and the risk that the sire (father) of the puppies is another breed entirely. And you won't be adding unwanted puppies to the already staggering pet population.

The health benefits of spaying your female by 6 months of age are outlined in the box on page 95. Spaying also eliminates the mess associated with seasonal bleeding and the problems involved with having to isolate your bitch for three to four weeks, twice a year, to keep her away from unneutered males. The female in heat has a strong desire to get to a male, and her scent will attract males from far and wide. A bitch in season cannot be allowed out of your sight for even a moment. Keeping her in a kennel run or wire crate is no guarantee that a male will not get to her. A dog can be very secretive and not show any indication of heat until she is mated by a male dog. You are best armed against such an event by spaying.

Spayed and neutered animals will not become fat and lazy unless you let them. About the time when spaying and neutering can be done, the dog is nearing maturity and needs an adjustment in the type and amount of food being

Spayed and neutered dogs will not become fat and lazy unless you let them.

served anyway. By keeping the diet appropriate to age and activity level, your dog will not get fat.

The only appropriate reason for keeping intact males or females is for breeding purposes, and animals kept for that purpose should be especially fine examples of the breed and qualify for registration with the JRTCA prior to breeding. They should be outstanding in quality, performance, and temperament, free from any known genetic defects, and possess the working instincts that have kept this dog what she is for so many years. Breeding known successful hunters is also suggested to keep the strong desire to hunt in the breed for the future.

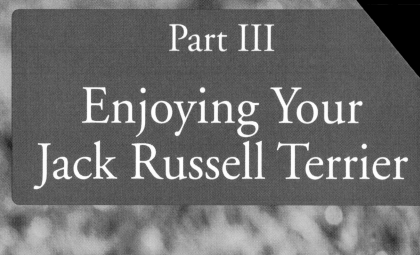

Part III

Enjoying Your Jack Russell Terrier

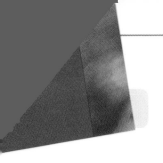

Training Your Jack Russell Terrier

by Peggy Moran

Training makes your best friend better! A properly trained dog has a happier life and a longer life expectancy. He is also more appreciated by the people he encounters each day, both at home and out and about.

A trained dog walks nicely and joins his family often, going places untrained dogs cannot go. When he meets people for the first time, he greets them by sitting and waiting to be petted, rather than jumping up. At home he doesn't compete with his human family, and alone he is not destructive or overly anxious. He isn't continually nagged with words like "no," since he has learned not to misbehave in the first place. He is never shamed, harshly punished, or treated unkindly, and he is a well-loved, involved member of the family.

Sounds good, doesn't it? If you are willing to invest some time, thought, and patience, the words above could soon be used to describe your dog (though perhaps changing "he" to "she"). Educating your pet in a positive way is fun and easy, and there is no better gift you can give your pet than the guarantee of improved understanding and a great relationship.

This chapter will explain how to offer kind leadership, reshape your pet's behavior in a positive and practical way, and even get a head start on simple obedience training.

Understanding Builds the Bond

Dog training is a learning adventure on both ends of the leash. Before attempting to teach their dog new behaviors or change unwanted ones, thoughtful dog owners take the time to understand why their pets behave the way they do, and how their own behavior can be either a positive or negative influence on their dog.

Canine Nature

Loving dogs as much as we do, it's easy to forget they are a completely different species. Despite sharing our homes and living as appreciated members of our families, dogs do not think or learn exactly the same way people do. Even if you love your dog like a child, you must remember to respect the fact that he is actually a dog.

Dogs have no idea when their behavior is inappropriate from a human perspective. They are not aware of the value of possessions they chew or of messes they make or the worry they sometimes seem to cause. While people tend to look at behavior as good and bad or right and wrong, dogs just discover what works and what doesn't work. Then they behave accordingly, learning from their own experiences and increasing or reducing behaviors to improve results for themselves.

You might wonder, "But don't dogs want to please us"? My answer is yes, provided your pleasure reflects back to them in positive ways they can feel and appreciate. Dogs do things for *dog* reasons, and everything they do works for them in some way or they wouldn't be doing it!

The Social Dog

Our pets descended from animals who lived in tightly knit, cooperative social groups. Though far removed in appearance and lifestyle from their ancestors, our dogs still relate in many of the same ways their wild relatives did. And in their relationships with one another, wild canids either lead or follow.

Canine ranking relationships are not about cruelty and power; they are about achievement and abilities. Competent dogs with high levels of drive and confidence step up, while deferring dogs step aside. But followers don't get the short end of the stick; they benefit from the security of having a more competent dog at the helm.

Our domestic dogs still measure themselves against other members of their group—us! Dog owners whose actions lead to positive results have willing, secure followers. But dogs may step up and fill the void or cut loose and do their own thing when their people fail to show capable leadership. When dogs are pushy, aggressive, and rude, or independent and unwilling, it's not because they have designs on the role of "master." It is more likely their owners failed to provide consistent leadership.

Dogs in training benefit from their handler's good leadership. Their education flows smoothly because they are impressed. Being in charge doesn't require you to physically dominate or punish your dog. You simply need to make some subtle changes in the way you relate to him every day.

Lead Your Pack!

Create schedules and structure daily activities. Dogs are creatures of habit and routines will create security. Feed meals at the same times each day and also try to schedule regular walks, training practices, and toilet outings. Your predictability will help your dog be patient.

Ask your dog to perform a task. Before releasing him to food or freedom, have him do something as simple as sit on command. Teach him that cooperation earns great results!

Give a release prompt (such as "let's go") when going through doors leading outside. This is a better idea than allowing your impatient pup to rush past you.

Pet your dog when he is calm, not when he is excited. Turn your touch into a tool that relaxes and settles.

Reward desirable rather than inappropriate behavior. Petting a jumping dog (who hasn't been invited up) reinforces jumping. Pet sitting dogs, and only invite lap dogs up after they've first "asked" by waiting for your invitation.

Replace personal punishment with positive reinforcement. Show a dog what *to do,* and motivate him to want to do it, and there will be no need to punish him for what he should *not do.* Dogs naturally follow, without the need for force or harshness.

Play creatively and appropriately. Your dog will learn the most about his social rank when he is playing with you. During play, dogs work to control toys and try to get the best of one another in a friendly way. The wrong sorts of play can create problems: For example, tug of war can lead to aggressiveness. Allowing your dog to control toys during play may result in possessive guarding when he has something he really values, such as a bone. Dogs who are chased during play may later run away from you when you approach to leash them. The right kinds of play will help increase your dog's social confidence while you gently assert your leadership.

How Dogs Learn (and How They Don't)

Dog training begins as a meeting of minds—yours and your dog's. Though the end goal may be to get your dog's body to behave in a specific way, training starts as a mind game. Your dog is learning all the time by observing the consequences of his actions and social interactions. He is always seeking out what he perceives as desirable and trying to avoid what he perceives as undesirable.

He will naturally repeat a behavior that either brings him more good stuff or makes bad stuff go away (these are both types of reinforcement). He will naturally avoid a behavior that brings him more bad stuff or makes the good stuff go away (these are both types of punishment).

Both reinforcement and punishment can be perceived as either the direct result of something the dog did himself, or as coming from an outside source.

Using Life's Rewards

Your best friend is smart and he is also cooperative. When the best things in life can only be had by working with you, your dog will view you as a facilitator. You unlock doors to all of the positively reinforcing experiences he values: his freedom, his friends at the park, food, affection, walks, and play. The trained dog accompanies you through those doors and waits to see what working with you will bring.

Rewarding your dog for good behavior is called positive reinforcement, and, as we've just seen, it increases the likelihood that he will repeat that behavior. The perfect reward is anything your dog wants that is safe and appropriate. Don't limit yourself to toys, treats, and things that come directly from you. Harness life's positives—barking at squirrels, chasing a falling leaf, bounding away from you at the dog park, pausing for a moment to sniff everything—and allow your dog to earn access to those things as rewards that come from cooperating with you. When he looks at you, when he sits, when he comes when you call—any prompted behavior can earn one of life's rewards. When he works with you, he earns the things he most appreciates; but when he tries to get those things on his own, he cannot. Rather than seeing you as someone who always says "no," your dog will view you as the one who says "let's go!" He will *want* to follow.

What About Punishment?

Not only is it unnecessary to personally punish dogs, it is abusive. No matter how convinced you are that your dog "knows right from wrong," in reality he will associate personal punishment with the punisher. The resulting cowering, "guilty"-looking postures are actually displays of submission and fear. Later,

Purely Positive Reinforcement

With positive training, we emphasize teaching dogs what they should do to earn reinforcements, rather than punishing them for unwanted behaviors.

- Focus on teaching "do" rather than "don't." For example, a sitting dog isn't jumping.
- Use positive reinforcers that are valuable to your dog and the situation: A tired dog values rest; a confined dog values freedom.
- Play (appropriately)!
- Be a consistent leader.
- Set your dog up for success by anticipating and preventing problems.
- Notice and reward desirable behavior, and give him lots of attention when he is being good.
- Train ethically. Use humane methods and equipment that do not frighten or hurt your dog.
- When you are angry, walk away and plan a positive strategy.
- Keep practice sessions short and sweet. Five to ten minutes, three to five times a day is best.

when the punisher isn't around and the coast is clear, the same behavior he was punished for—such as raiding a trash can—might bring a self-delivered, very tasty result. The punished dog hasn't learned not to misbehave; he has learned to not get caught.

Does punishment ever have a place in dog training? Many people will heartily insist it does not. But dog owners often get frustrated as they try to stick to the path of all-positive reinforcement. It sure sounds great, but is it realistic, or even natural, to *never* say "no" to your dog?

A wild dog's life is not *all* positive. Hunger and thirst are both examples of negative reinforcement; the resulting discomfort motivates the wild dog to seek food and water. He encounters natural aversives such as pesky insects; mats in his coat; cold days; rainy days; sweltering hot days; and occasional run-ins with thorns, brambles, skunks, bees, and other nastiness. These all affect his behavior, as he tries to avoid the bad stuff whenever possible. The wild dog also occasionally encounters social punishers from others in his group when he gets too pushy. Starting with a growl or a snap from Mom, and later some mild and ritualized discipline from other members of his four-legged family, he learns to modify behaviors that elicit grouchy responses.

Our pet dogs don't naturally experience all positive results either, because they learn from their surroundings and from social experiences with other dogs. Watch a group of pet dogs playing together and you'll see a very old educational system still being used. As they wrestle and attempt to assert themselves, you'll notice many mouth-on-neck moments. Their playful biting is inhibited, with no intention to cause harm, but their message is clear: "Say uncle or this could hurt more!"

Observing that punishment does occur in nature, some people may feel compelled to try to be like the big wolf with their pet dogs. Becoming aggressive or heavy-handed with your pet will backfire! Your dog will not be impressed, nor will he want to follow you. Punishment causes dogs to change their behavior to avoid or escape discomfort and threats. Threatened dogs will either become very passive and offer submissive, appeasing postures, attempt to flee, or rise to the occasion and fight back. When people personally punish their dogs in an angry manner, one of these three defensive mechanisms will be triggered. Which one depends on a dog's genetic temperament as well as his past social experiences. Since we don't want to make our pets feel the need to avoid or escape us, personal punishment has no place in our training.

Remote Consequences

Sometimes, however, all-positive reinforcement is just not enough. That's because not all reinforcement comes from us. An inappropriate behavior can be self-reinforcing—just doing it makes the dog feel better in some way, whether you are there to say "good boy!" or not. Some examples are eating garbage, pulling the stuffing out of your sofa, barking at passersby, or urinating on the floor.

Although you don't want to personally punish your dog, the occasional deterrent may be called for to help derail these kinds of self-rewarding misbehaviors. In these cases, mild forms of impersonal or remote punishment can be used as part of a correction. The goal isn't to make your dog feel bad or to "know he has done wrong," but to help redirect him to alternate behaviors that are more acceptable to you.

The Problems with Personal Punishment

- Personally punished dogs are not taught appropriate behaviors.
- Personally punished dogs only stop misbehaving when they are caught or interrupted, but they don't learn not to misbehave when they are alone.
- Personally punished dogs become shy, fearful, and distrusting.
- Personally punished dogs may become defensively aggressive.
- Personally punished dogs become suppressed and inhibited.
- Personally punished dogs become stressed, triggering stress-reducing behaviors that their owners interpret as acts of spite, triggering even more punishment.
- Personally punished dogs have stressed owners.
- Personally punished dogs may begin to repeat behaviors they have been taught will result in negative, but predictable, attention.
- Personally punished dogs are more likely to be given away than are positively trained dogs.

You do this by pairing a slightly startling, totally impersonal sound with an equally impersonal and *very mild* remote consequence. The impersonal sound might be a single shake of an empty plastic pop bottle with pennies in it, held out of your dog's sight. Or you could use a vocal expression such as "eh!" delivered with you looking *away* from your misbehaving dog.

Pair your chosen sound—the penny bottle or "eh!"—with either a slight tug on his collar or a sneaky spritz on the rump from a water bottle. Do this right *as* he touches something he should not; bad timing will confuse your dog and undermine your training success.

To keep things under your control and make sure you get the timing right, it's best to do this as a setup. "Accidentally" drop a shoe on the floor, and then help your dog learn some things are best avoided. As he sniffs the shoe say "eh!" without looking at him and give a *slight* tug against his collar. This sound will quickly become meaningful as a correction all by itself—sometimes after just one setup—making the tug correction obsolete. The tug lets your dog see that you were right; going for that shoe *was* a bad idea! Your wise dog will be more likely to heed your warning next time, and probably move closer to you where it's safe. Be a good friend and pick up the nasty shoe. He'll be relieved and you'll look heroic. Later, when he's home alone and encounters a stray shoe, he'll want to give it a wide berth.

Your negative marking sound will come in handy in the future, when your dog begins to venture down the wrong behavioral path. The goal is not to announce your disapproval or to threaten your dog. You are not telling him to stop or showing how *you* feel about his behavior. You are sounding a warning to a friend who's venturing off toward danger—"I wouldn't if I were you!" Suddenly, there is an abrupt, rather startling, noise! Now is the moment to redirect him and help him earn positive reinforcement. That interrupted behavior will become something he wants to avoid in the future, but he won't want to avoid you.

Practical Commands for Family Pets

Before you begin training your dog, let's look at some equipment you'll want to have on hand:

- **A buckle collar** is fine for most dogs. If your dog pulls *very* hard, try a head collar, a device similar to a horse halter that helps reduce pulling by turning the dog's head. *Do not* use a choke chain (sometimes called a training collar), because they cause physical harm even when used correctly.
- **Six-foot training leash and twenty-six–foot retractable leash.**
- **A few empty plastic soda bottles with about twenty pennies in each one.** This will be used to impersonally interrupt misbehaviors before redirecting dogs to more positive activities.
- **A favorite squeaky toy,** to motivate, attract attention, and reward your dog during training.

Lure your dog to take just a few steps with you on the leash by being inviting and enthusiastic. Make sure you reward him for his efforts.

Baby Steps

Allow your young pup to drag a short, lightweight leash attached to a buckle collar for a few *supervised* moments, several times each day. At first the leash may annoy him and he may jump around a bit trying to get away from it. Distract him with your squeaky toy or a bit of his kibble and he'll quickly get used to his new "tail."

Begin walking him on the leash by holding the end and following him. As he adapts, you can begin to assert gentle direct pressure to teach him to follow you. Don't jerk or yank, or he will become afraid to walk when the leash is on. If he becomes hesitant, squat down facing him and let him figure out that by moving toward you he is safe and secure. If he remains confused or frightened and doesn't come to you, go to him and help him understand that you provide safe harbor while he's on the leash. Then back away a few steps and try again to lure him to you. As he learns that you are the "home base," he'll want to follow when you walk a few steps, waiting for you to stop, squat down, and make him feel great.

So Attached to You!

The next step in training your dog—and this is a very important one—is to begin spending at least an hour or more each day with him on a four- to six-foot leash, held by or tethered to you. This training will increase his attachment to you—literally!—as you sit quietly or walk about, tending to your household business. When you are quiet, he'll learn it is time to settle; when you are active, he'll learn to move with you. Tethering also keeps him out of trouble when you are busy but still want his company. It is a great alternative to confining a dog, and can be used instead of crating any time you're home and need to slow him down a bit.

Rotating your dog from supervised freedom to tethered time to some quiet time in the crate or his gated area gives him a diverse and balanced day while he is learning. Two confined or tethered hours is the most you should require of your dog in one stretch, before changing to some supervised freedom, play, or a walk.

The dog in training may, at times, be stressed by all of the changes he is dealing with. Provide a stress outlet, such as a toy to chew on, when he is confined or tethered. He will settle into his quiet time more quickly and completely. Always be sure to provide several rounds of daily play and free time (in a fenced area or on your retractable leash) in addition to plenty of chewing materials.

Dog Talk

Dogs don't speak in words, but they do have a language—body language. They use postures, vocalizations, movements, facial gestures,

Tethering your dog is great way to keep him calm and under control, but still with you.

odors, and touch—usually with their mouths—to communicate what they are feeling and thinking.

We also "speak" using body language. We have quite an array of postures, movements, and facial gestures that accompany our touch and language as we attempt to communicate with our pets. And our dogs can quickly figure us out!

Alone, without associations, words are just noises. But, because we pair them with meaningful body language, our dogs make the connection. Dogs can really learn to understand much of what we *say,* if what we *do* at the same time is consistent.

The Positive Marker

Start your dog's education with one of the best tricks in dog training: Pair various positive reinforcers—food, a toy, touch—with a sound such as a click on a clicker (which you can get at the pet supply store) or a spoken word like "good!" or "yes!" This will enable you to later "mark" your dog's desirable behaviors.

It seems too easy: Just say "yes!" and give the dog his toy. (Or use whatever sound and reward you have chosen.) Later, when you make your marking sound right at the instant your dog does the right thing, he will know you are going to be giving him something good for that particular action. And he'll be eager to repeat the behavior to hear you mark it again!

Next, you must teach your dog to understand the meaning of cues you'll be using to ask him to perform specific behaviors. This is easy, too. Does he already do things you might like him to do on command? Of course! He lies down, he sits, he picks things up, he drops them again, he comes to you. All of the behaviors you'd like to control are already part of your dog's natural repertoire. The trick is getting him to offer those behaviors when you ask for them. And that means you have to teach him to associate a particular behavior on his part with a particular behavior on your part.

Sit Happens

Teach your dog an important new rule: From now on, he is only touched and petted when he is either sitting or lying down. You won't need to ask him to sit; in fact, you should not. Just keeping him tethered near you so there isn't much to do but stand, be ignored, or settle, and wait until sit happens.

He may pester you a bit, but be stoic and unresponsive. Starting now, when *you* are sitting down, a sitting dog is the only one you see and pay attention to. He will eventually sit, and as he does, attach the word "sit"—but don't be too excited or he'll jump right back up. Now mark with your positive sound that promises something good, then reward him with a slow, quiet, settling pet.

Training requires consistent reinforcement. Ask others to also wait until your dog is sitting and calm to touch him, and he will associate being petted with being relaxed. Be sure you train your dog to associate everyone's touch with quiet bonding.

Reinforcing "Sit" as a Command

Since your dog now understands one concept of working for a living—sit to earn petting—you can begin to shape and reinforce his desire to sit. Hold toys, treats, his bowl of food, and turn into a statue. But don't prompt him to sit! Instead, remain frozen and unavailable, looking somewhere out into space, over his head. He will put on a bit of a show, trying to get a response from you, and may offer various behaviors, but only one will push your button—sitting. Wait for him to offer the "right" behavior, and when he does, you unfreeze. Say "sit," then mark with an excited "good!" and give him the toy or treat with a release command—"OK!"

When you notice spontaneous sits occurring, be sure to take advantage of those free opportunities to make your command sequence meaningful and positive. Say "sit" as you observe sit happen—then mark with "good!" and praise, pet, or reward the dog. Soon, every time you look at your dog he'll be sitting and looking right back at you!

Now, after thirty days of purely positive practice, it's time to give him a test. When he is just walking around doing his own thing, suddenly ask him to sit. He'll probably do it right away. If he doesn't, do *not* repeat your command, or you'll just undermine its meaning ("sit" means sit *now;* the command is not "sit, sit, sit, sit"). Instead, get something he likes and let him know you have it. Wait for him to offer the sit—he will—then say "sit!" and complete your marking and rewarding sequence.

OK

"OK" will probably rate as one of your dog's favorite words. It's like the word "recess" to schoolchildren. It is the word used to release your dog from a command. You can introduce "OK" during your "sit" practice. When he gets up from a sit, say "OK" to tell him the sitting is finished. Soon that sound will mean "freedom."

Make it even more meaningful and positive. Whenever he spontaneously bounds away, say "OK!" Squeak a toy, and when he notices and shows interest, toss it for him.

Down

I've mentioned that you should only pet your dog when he is either sitting or lying down. Now, using the approach I've just introduced for "sit," teach your dog to lie down. You will be a statue, and hold something he would like to get but that you'll only release to a dog who is lying down. It helps to lower the desired item to the floor in front of him, still not speaking and not letting him have it until he offers you the new behavior you are seeking.

Lower your dog's reward to the floor to help him figure out what behavior will earn him his reward.

He may offer a sit and then wait expectantly, but you must make him keep searching for the new trick that triggers your generosity. Allow your dog to experiment and find the right answer, even if he has to search around for it first. When he lands on "down" and learns it is another behavior that works, he'll offer it more quickly the next time.

Don't say "down" until he lies down, to tightly associate your prompt with the correct behavior. To say "down, down, down" as he is sitting, looking at you, or pawing at the toy would make "down" mean those behaviors instead! Whichever behavior he offers, a training opportunity has been created. Once you've attached and shaped both sitting and lying down, you can ask for both behaviors with your verbal prompts, "sit" or "down." Be sure to only reinforce the "correct" reply!

Stay

"Stay" can easily be taught as an extension of what you've already been practicing. To teach "stay," you follow the entire sequence for reinforcing a "sit" or "down," except you wait a bit longer before you give the release word, "OK!" Wait a second or two longer during each practice before saying "OK!" and releasing your dog to the positive reinforcer (toy, treat, or one of life's other rewards).

You can step on the leash to help your dog understand the down-stay, but only do this when he is already lying down. You don't want to hurt him!

If he gets up before you've said "OK," you have two choices: pretend the release was your idea and quickly interject "OK!" as he breaks; or, if he is more experienced and practiced, mark the behavior with your correction sound— "eh!"— and then gently put him back on the spot, wait for him to lie down, and begin again. Be sure the next three practices are a success. Ask him to wait for just a second, and release him before he can be wrong. You need to keep your dog feeling like more of a success than a failure as you begin to test his training in increasingly more distracting and difficult situations.

As he gets the hang of it—he stays until you say "OK"—you can gradually push for longer times—up to a minute on a sit-stay, and up to three minutes on a down-stay. You can also gradually add distractions and work in new environments. To add a minor self-correction for the down-stay, stand on the dog's leash after he lies down, allowing about three inches of slack. If tries to get up before you've said "OK," he'll discover it doesn't work.

Do not step on the leash to make your dog lie down! This could badly hurt his neck, and will destroy his trust in you. Remember, we are teaching our dogs to make the best choices, not inflicting our answers upon them!

Come

Rather than thinking of "come" as an action—"come to me"—think of it as a place—"the dog is sitting in front of me, facing me." Since your dog by now really likes sitting to earn your touch and other positive reinforcement, he's likely to sometimes sit directly in front of you, facing you, all on his own. When this happens, give it a specific name: "come."

Now follow the rest of the training steps you have learned to make him like doing it and reinforce the behavior by practicing it any chance you get. Anything your dog wants and likes could be earned as a result of his first offering the sit-in-front known as "come."

You can help guide him into the right location. Use your hands as "landing gear" and pat the insides of your legs at his nose level. Do this while backing up a bit, to help him maneuver to the straight-in-front, facing-you position. Don't say the

Pat the insides of your legs to show your dog exactly where you like him to sit when you say "come."

word "come" while he's maneuvering, because he hasn't! You are trying to make "come" the end result, not the work in progress.

You can also help your dog by marking his movement in the right direction: Use your positive sound or word to promise he is getting warm. When he finally sits facing you, enthusiastically say "come," mark again with your positive word, and release him with an enthusiastic "OK!" Make it so worth his while, with lots of play and praise, that he can't wait for you to ask him to come again!

Building a Better Recall

Practice, practice, practice. Now, practice some more. Teach your dog that all good things in life hinge upon him first sitting in front of you in a behavior named "come." When you think he really has got it, test him by asking him to "come" as you gradually add distractions and change locations. Expect setbacks as you make these changes and practice accordingly. Lower your expectations and make his task easier so he is able to get it right. Use those distractions as rewards, when they are appropriate. For example, let him check out the interesting leaf that blew by as a reward for first coming to you and ignoring it.

Add distance and call your dog to come while he is on his retractable leash. If he refuses and sits looking at you blankly, *do not* jerk, tug, "pop," or reel him in. Do nothing! It is his move; wait to see what behavior he offers. He'll either begin to approach (mark the behavior with an excited "good!"), sit and do nothing (just keep waiting), or he'll try to move in some direction other than toward you. If he tries to leave, use your correction marker—"eh!"— and bring him to a stop by letting him walk to the end of the leash, *not* by jerking him. Now walk to him in a neutral manner, and don't jerk or show any disapproval. Gently bring him back to the spot where he was when you called him, then back away and face him, still waiting and not reissuing your command. Let him keep examining his options until he finds the one that works—yours!

If you have practiced everything I've suggested so far and given your dog a chance to really learn what "come" means, he is well aware of what you want and is quite intelligently weighing all his options. The only way he'll know your way is the one that works is to be allowed to examine his other choices and discover that they *don't* work.

Sooner or later every dog tests his training. Don't be offended or angry when your dog tests you. No matter how positive you've made it, he won't always want to do everything you ask, every time. When he explores the "what happens if I don't" scenario, your training is being strengthened. He will discover through his own process of trial and error that the best—and only—way out of a command he really doesn't feel compelled to obey is to obey it.

Let's Go

Many pet owners wonder if they can retain control while walking their dogs and still allow at least some running in front, sniffing, and playing. You might worry that allowing your dog occasional freedom could result in him expecting it all the time, leading to a testy, leash-straining walk. It's possible for both parties on the leash to have an enjoyable experience by implementing and reinforcing well-thought-out training techniques.

Begin by making word associations you'll use on your walks. Give the dog some slack on the leash, and as he starts to walk away from you say "OK" and begin to follow him.

Do not let him drag you; set the pace even when he is being given a turn at being the leader. Whenever he starts to pull, just come to a standstill and refuse to move (or refuse to allow him to continue forward) until there is slack in the leash. Do this correction without saying anything at all. When he isn't pulling, you may decide to just stand still and let him sniff about within the range the slack leash allows, or you may even mosey along following him. After a few minutes of "recess," it is time to work. Say something like "that's it" or "time's up," close the distance between you and your dog, and touch him.

Next say "let's go" (or whatever command you want to use to mean "follow me as we walk"). Turn and walk off, and, if he follows, mark his behavior with "good!" Then stop,

Give your dog slack on his leash as you walk and let him make the decision to walk with you.

When your dog catches up with you, make sure you let him know what a great dog he is!

Intersperse periods of attentive walking, where your dog is on a shorter leash, with periods on a slack leash, where he is allowed to look and sniff around.

squat down, and let him catch you. Make him glad he did! Start again, and do a few transitions as he gets the hang of your follow-the-leader game, speeding up, slowing down, and trying to make it fun. When you stop, he gets to catch up and receive some deserved positive reinforcement. Don't forget that's the reason he is following you, so be sure to make it worth his while!

Require him to remain attentive to you. Do not allow sniffing, playing, eliminating, or pulling during your time as leader on a walk. If he seems to get distracted—which, by the way, is the main reason dogs walk poorly with their people—change direction or pace without saying a word. Just help him realize "oops, I lost track of my human." Do not jerk his neck and say "heel"—this will make the word "heel" mean pain in the neck and will not encourage him to cooperate with you. Don't repeat "let's go," either. He needs to figure out that it is his job to keep track of and follow you if he wants to earn the positive benefits you provide.

The best reward you can give a dog for performing an attentive, controlled walk is a few minutes of walking without all of the controls. Of course, he must remain on a leash even during the "recess" parts of the walk, but allowing him to discriminate between attentive following—"let's go"—and having a few moments of relaxation—"OK"—will increase his willingness to work.

Training for Attention

Your dog pretty much has a one-track mind. Once he is focused on something, everything else is excluded. This can be great, for instance, when he's focusing on you! But it can also be dangerous if, for example, his attention is riveted on the bunny he is chasing and he does not hear you call—that is, not unless he has been trained to pay attention when you say his name.

When you say your dog's name, you'll want him to make eye contact with you. Begin teaching this by making yourself so intriguing that he can't help but look.

When you call your dog's name, you will again be seeking a specific response—eye contact. The best way to teach this is to trigger his alerting response by making a noise with your mouth, such as whistling or a kissing sound, and then immediately doing something he'll find very intriguing.

You can play a treasure hunt game to help teach him to regard his name as a request for attention. As a bonus, you can reinforce the rest of his new vocabulary at the same time.

Treasure Hunt

Make a kissing sound, then jump up and find a dog toy or dramatically raid the fridge and rather noisily eat a piece of cheese. After doing this twice, make a kissing sound and then look at your dog.

Of course he is looking at you! He is waiting to see if that sound—the kissing sound—means you're going to go hunting again. After all, you're so good at it! Because he is looking, say his name, mark with "good," then go hunting and find his toy. Release it to him with an "OK." At any point if he follows you, attach your "let's go!" command; if he leaves you, give permission with "OK."

Using this approach, he cannot be wrong—any behavior your dog offers can be named. You can add things like "take it" when he picks up a toy, and "thank you" when he happens to drop one. Many opportunities to make your new vocabulary meaningful and positive can be found within this simple training game.

Problems to watch out for when teaching the treasure hunt:

- You really do not want your dog to come to you when you call his name (later, when you try to engage his attention to ask him to stay, he'll already be on his way toward you). You just want him to look at you.
- Saying "watch me, watch me" doesn't teach your dog to *offer* his attention. It just makes you a background noise.
- Don't lure your dog's attention with the reward. Get his attention and then reward him for looking. Try holding a toy in one hand with your arm stretched out to your side. Wait until he looks at you rather than the toy. Now say his name then mark with "good!" and release the toy. As he goes for it, say "OK."

To get your dog's attention, try holding his toy with your arm out to your side. Wait until he looks at you, then mark the moment and give him the toy.

Teaching Cooperation

Never punish your dog for failing to obey you or try to punish him into compliance. Bribing, repeating yourself, and doing a behavior for him all avoid the real issue of dog training—his will. He must be helped to be willing, not made to achieve tasks. Good dog training helps your dog want to obey. He learns that he can gain what he values most through cooperation and compliance, and can't gain those things any other way.

Your dog is learning to *earn,* rather than expect, the good things in life. And you've become much more important to him than you were before. Because you are allowing him to experiment and learn, he doesn't have to be forced, manipulated, or bribed. When he wants something, he can gain it by cooperating with you. One of those "somethings"—and a great reward you shouldn't underestimate—is your positive attention, paid to him with love and sincere approval!

Chapter 10

Housetraining Your Jack Russell Terrier

Excerpted from Housetraining:
An Owner's Guide to a Happy
Healthy Pet, 1st Edition,
by September Morn

By the time puppies are about 3 weeks old, they start to follow their mother around. When they are a few steps away from their clean sleeping area, the mama dog stops. The pups try to nurse but mom won't allow it. The pups mill around in frustration, then nature calls and they all urinate and defecate here, away from their bed. The mother dog returns to the nest, with her brood waddling behind her. Their first housetraining lesson has been a success.

The next one to housetrain puppies should be their breeder. The breeder watches as the puppies eliminate, then deftly removes the soiled papers and replaces them with clean papers before the pups can traipse back through their messes. He has wisely arranged the puppies' space so their bed, food, and drinking water are as far away from the elimination area as possible. This way, when the pups follow their mama, they will move away from their sleeping and eating area before eliminating. This habit will help the pups be easily housetrained.

Your Housetraining Shopping List

While your puppy's mother and breeder are getting her started on good housetraining habits, you'll need to do some shopping. If you have all the essentials in place before your dog arrives, it will be easier to help her learn the rules from day one.

Newspaper: The younger your puppy and larger her breed, the more newspapers you'll need. Newspaper is absorbent, abundant, cheap, and convenient.

Puddle Pads: If you prefer not to stockpile newspaper, a commercial alternative is puddle pads. These thick paper pads can be purchased under several trade names at pet supply stores. The pads have waterproof backing, so puppy urine doesn't seep through onto the floor. Their disadvantages are that they will cost you more than newspapers and that they contain plastics that are not biodegradable.

Poop Removal Tool: There are several types of poop removal tools available. Some are designed with a separate pan and rake, and others have the handles hinged like scissors. Some scoops need two hands for operation, while others are designed for one-handed use. Try out the different brands at your pet supply store. Put a handful of pebbles or dog kibble on the floor and then pick them up with each type of scoop to determine which works best for you.

Plastic Bags: When you take your dog outside your yard, you *must* pick up after her. Dog waste is unsightly, smelly, and can harbor disease. In many cities and towns, the law mandates dog owners clean up pet waste deposited on public ground. Picking up after your dog using a plastic bag scoop is simple. Just put your hand inside the bag, like a mitten, and then grab the droppings. Turn the bag inside out, tie the top, and that's that.

Crate: To housetrain a puppy, you will need some way to confine her when you're unable to supervise. A dog crate is a secure way to confine your dog for short periods during the day and to use as a comfortable bed at night. Crates come in wire mesh and in plastic. The wire ones are foldable to store flat in a smaller space. The plastic ones are more cozy, draft-free, and quiet, and are approved for airline travel.

Baby Gates: Since you shouldn't crate a dog for more than an hour or two at a time during the day, baby gates are a good way to limit your dog's freedom in the house. Be sure the baby gates you use are safe. The old-fashioned wooden, expanding lattice type has seriously injured a number of children by collapsing and trapping a leg, arm, or neck. That type of gate can hurt a puppy, too, so use the modern grid type gates instead. You'll need more than one baby gate if you have several doorways to close off.

Exercise Pen: Portable exercise pens are great when you have a young pup or a small dog. These metal or plastic pens are made of rectangular panels that are hinged together. The pens are freestanding, sturdy, foldable, and can be carried like a suitcase. You could set one up in your kitchen as the pup's daytime corral, and then take it outdoors to contain your pup while you garden or just sit and enjoy the day.

Enzymatic Cleaner: All dogs make housetraining mistakes. Accept this and be ready for it by buying an enzymatic cleaner made especially for pet accidents. Dogs like to eliminate where they have done it before, and lingering smells lead them to those spots. Ordinary household cleaners may remove all the odors you can smell, but only an enzymatic cleaner will remove everything your dog can smell.

The First Day

Housetraining is a matter of establishing good habits in your dog. That means you never want her to learn anything she will eventually have to unlearn. Start off housetraining on the right foot by teaching your dog that you prefer her to eliminate outside. Designate a potty area in your backyard (if you have one) or

A crate will be your dog's overnight bed and her safe haven both at home and when you are away.

Don't Overuse the Crate

A crate serves well as a dog's overnight bed, but you should not leave the dog in her crate for more than an hour or two during the day. Throughout the day, she needs to play and exercise. She is likely to want to drink some water and will undoubtedly eliminate. Confining your dog all day will give her no option but to soil her crate. This is not just unpleasant for you and the dog, but it reinforces bad cleanliness habits. And crating a pup for the whole day is abusive. Don't do it.

in the street in front of your home and take your dog to it as soon as you arrive home. Let her sniff a bit and, when she squats to go, give the action a name: "potty" or "do it" or anything else you won't be embarrassed to say in public. Eventually your dog will associate that word with the act and will eliminate on command. When she's finished, praise her with "good potty!"

That first day, take your puppy out to the potty area frequently. Although she may not eliminate every time, you are establishing a routine: You take her to her spot, ask her to eliminate, and praise her when she does.

Just before bedtime, take your dog to her potty area once more. Stand by and wait until she produces. Do not put your dog to bed for the night until she has eliminated. Be patient and calm. This is not the time to play with or excite your dog. If she's too excited, a pup not only won't eliminate, she probably won't want to sleep either.

Most dogs, even young ones, will not soil their beds if they can avoid it. For this reason, a sleeping crate can be a tremendous help during housetraining. Being crated at night can help a dog develop the muscles that control elimination. So after your dog has emptied out, put her to bed in her crate.

A good place to put your dog's sleeping crate is near your own bed. Dogs are pack animals, so they feel safer sleeping with others in a common area. In your bedroom, the pup will be near you and you'll be close enough to hear when she wakes during the night and needs to eliminate.

Pups under 4 months old often are not able to hold their urine all night. If your puppy has settled down to sleep but awakens and fusses a few hours later, she probably needs to go out. For the best housetraining progress, take your pup to her elimination area whenever she needs to go, even in the wee hours of the morning.

Your pup may soil in her crate if you ignore her late night urgency. It's unfair to let this happen, and it sends the wrong message about your expectations for cleanliness. Resign yourself to this midnight outing and just get up and take the pup out. Your pup will outgrow this need soon and will learn in the process that she can count on you, and you'll wake happily each morning to a clean dog.

The next morning, the very first order of business is to take your pup out to eliminate. Don't forget to take her to her special potty spot, ask her to eliminate, and then praise her when she does. After your pup empties out in the morning, give her breakfast, and then take her to her potty area again. After that, she shouldn't need to eliminate again right away, so you can allow her some free playtime. Keep an eye on the pup though, because when she pauses in play she may need to go potty. Take her to the right spot, give the command, and praise if she produces.

Confine Your Pup

A pup or dog who has not finished housetraining should *never* be allowed the run of the house unattended. A new dog (especially a puppy) with unlimited access to your house will make her own choices about where to eliminate. Vigilance during your new dog's first few weeks in your home will pay big dividends. Every potty mistake delays housetraining progress; every success speeds it along.

Prevent problems by setting up a controlled environment for your new pet. A good place for a puppy corral is often the kitchen. Kitchens almost always have waterproof or easily cleaned floors, which is a distinct asset with leaky pups. A bathroom, laundry room, or enclosed porch could be used for a puppy corral, but the kitchen is generally the best location. Kitchens are a meeting place and a hub of activity for many families, and a puppy will learn better manners when she is socialized thoroughly with family, friends, and nice strangers.

The way you structure your pup's corral area is very important. Her bed, food, and water should be at the opposite end of the corral from the potty area. When you first get your pup, spread newspaper over the rest of the floor of her playpen corral. Lay the papers at least four pages thick and be sure to overlap the edges. As you note the pup's progress, you can remove the papers nearest the sleeping and eating corner. Gradually decrease the size of the papered area until only the end where you want the pup to eliminate is covered. If you will be training your dog to eliminate outside, place newspaper at the end of the corral that is closest to the door that leads outdoors. That way as she moves away from the clean area to the papered area, the pup will also form the habit of heading toward the door to go out.

Maintain a scent marker for the pup's potty area by reserving a small soiled piece of paper when you clean up. Place this piece, with her scent of urine, under the top sheet of the clean papers you spread. This will cue your pup where to eliminate.

Most dog owners use a combination of indoor papers and outdoor elimination areas. When the pup is left by herself in the corral, she can potty on the ever-present newspaper. When you are available to take the pup outside, she can do her business in the outdoor spot. It is not difficult to switch a pup from indoor paper training to outdoor

A dog who is not reliably housetrained should never have free run of the house.

elimination. Owners of large pups often switch early, but potty papers are still useful if the pup spends time in her indoor corral while you're away. Use the papers as long as your pup needs them. If you come home and they haven't been soiled, you are ahead.

When setting up your pup's outdoor yard, put the lounging area as far away as possible from the potty area, just as with the indoor corral setup. People with large yards, for example, might leave a patch unmowed at the edge of the lawn to serve as the dog's elimination area. Other dog owners teach the dog to relieve herself in a designated corner of a deck or patio. For an apartment-dwelling city dog, the outdoor potty area might be a tiny balcony or the curb. Each dog owner has somewhat different expectations for their dog. Teach your dog to eliminate in a spot that suits your environment and lifestyle.

Be sure to pick up droppings in your yard at least once a day. Dogs have a natural desire to stay far away from their own excrement, and if too many piles litter the ground, your dog won't want to walk through it and will start eliminating elsewhere. Leave just one small piece of feces in the potty area to remind your dog where the right spot is located.

To help a pup adapt to the change from indoors to outdoors, take one of her potty papers outside to the new elimination area. Let the pup stand on the paper when she goes potty outdoors. Each day for four days, reduce the size of the paper by half. By the fifth day, the pup, having used a smaller and smaller piece of paper to stand on, will probably just go to that spot and eliminate.

A young puppy will need very frequent potty trips.

Take your pup to her outdoor potty place frequently throughout the day. A puppy can hold her urine for only about as many hours as her age in months, and will move her bowels as many times a day as she eats. So a 2-month-old pup will urinate about every two hours, while at 4 months she can manage about four hours between piddles. Pups vary somewhat in their rate of development, so this is not a hard and fast rule. It does, however, present a realistic idea of how long a pup can be left without access to a potty place. Past 4 months, her potty trips will be less frequent.

When you take the dog outdoors to her spot, keep her leashed so that she won't wander away. Stand quietly and let her sniff around in the designated area. If your pup starts to leave before she has eliminated, gently lead her back and remind her to go. If your pup sniffs at the spot, praise her calmly, say the command word, and just wait. If she produces, praise serenely, then give her time to sniff around a little more. She may not be finished, so give her time to go again before allowing her to play and explore her new home.

If you find yourself waiting more than five minutes for your dog to potty, take her back inside. Watch your pup carefully for twenty minutes, not giving her any opportunity to slip away to eliminate unnoticed. If you are too busy to watch the pup, put her in her crate. After twenty minutes, take her to the outdoor potty spot again and tell her what to do. If you're unsuccessful after five minutes, crate the dog again. Give her another chance to eliminate in fifteen or twenty minutes. Eventually, she will have to go.

Watch Your Pup

Be vigilant and don't let the pup make a mistake in the house. Each time you successfully anticipate elimination and take your pup to the potty spot, you'll move a step closer to your goal. Stay aware of your puppy's needs. If you ignore the pup, she will make mistakes and you'll be cleaning up more messes.

Keep a chart of your new dog's elimination behavior for the first three or four days. Jot down what times she eats, sleeps, and eliminates. After several days a pattern will emerge that can help you determine your pup's body rhythms. Most dogs tend to eliminate at fairly regular intervals. Once you know your new dog's natural rhythms, you'll be able to anticipate her needs and schedule appropriate potty outings.

Understanding the meanings of your dog's postures can also help you win the battle of the puddle. When your dog is getting ready to eliminate, she will display a specific set of postures. The sooner you can learn to read these signals, the cleaner your floor will stay.

A young puppy who feels the urge to eliminate may start to sniff the ground and walk in a circle. If the pup is very young, she may simply squat and go. All young puppies, male or female, squat to urinate. If you are housetraining a pup under 4 months of age, regardless of sex, watch for the beginnings of a squat as the signal to rush the pup to the potty area.

When a puppy is getting ready to defecate, she may run urgently back and forth or turn in a circle while sniffing or starting to squat. If defecation is imminent, the pup's anus may protrude or open slightly. When she starts to go, the pup will squat and hunch her back, her tail sticking straight out behind. There is no mistaking this posture; nothing else looks like this. If your pup takes this position, take her to her potty area. Hurry! You may have to carry her to get there in time.

A young puppy won't have much time between feeling the urge and actually eliminating, so you'll have to be quick to note her postural clues and intercept your pup in time. Pups

> ### TIP
>
> #### Water
>
> Make sure your dog has access to clean water at all times. Limiting the amount of water a dog drinks is not necessary for housetraining success and can be very dangerous. A dog needs water to digest food, to maintain a proper body temperature and proper blood volume, and to clean her system of toxins and wastes. A healthy dog will automatically drink the right amount. Do not restrict water intake. Controlling your dog's access to water is not the key to housetraining her; controlling her access to everything else in your home is.

The older the dog, the more obvious the signals that she needs to go.

from 3 to 6 months have a few seconds more between the urge and the act than younger ones do. The older your pup, the more time you'll have to get her to the potty area after she begins the posture signals that alert you to her need.

Accidents Happen

If you see your pup about to eliminate somewhere other than the designated area, interrupt her immediately. Say "wait, wait, wait!" or clap your hands loudly to startle her into stopping. Carry the pup, if she's still small enough, or take her collar and lead her to the correct area. Once your dog is in the potty area, give her the command to eliminate. Use a friendly voice for the command, then wait patiently for her to produce. The pup may be tense because you've just startled her and may have to relax a bit before she's able to eliminate. When she does her job, include the command word in the praise you give ("good potty").

The old-fashioned way of housetraining involved punishing a dog's mistakes even before she knew what she was supposed to do. Puppies were punished for breaking rules they didn't understand about functions they couldn't control. This was not fair. While your dog is new to housetraining, there is no need or excuse for punishing her mistakes. Your job is to take the dog to the potty area just before she needs to go, especially with pups under 3 months old. If you aren't watching your pup closely enough and she has an accident, don't punish the puppy for your failure to anticipate her needs. It's not the pup's fault; it's yours.

In any case, punishment is not an effective tool for housetraining most dogs. Many will react to punishment by hiding puddles and feces where you won't find them right away (like behind the couch or under the desk). This eventually may lead to punishment after the fact, which leads to more hiding, and so on.

Instead of punishing for mistakes, stay a step ahead of potty accidents by learning to anticipate your pup's needs. Accompany your dog to the designated potty area when she needs to go. Tell her what you want her to do and praise her when she goes. This will work wonders. Punishment won't be necessary if you are a good teacher.

What happens if you come upon a mess after the fact? Some trainers say a dog can't remember having eliminated, even a few moments after she has done so. This is not true. The fact is that urine and feces carry a dog's unique scent, which she (and every other dog) can instantly recognize. So, if you happen upon a potty mistake after the fact you can still use it to teach your dog.

But remember, no punishment! Spanking, hitting, shaking, or scaring a puppy for having a housetraining accident is confusing and counterproductive. Spend your energy instead on positive forms of teaching.

Praising your pup every time she eliminates in the right place will help her remember what you want her to do.

Take your pup and a paper towel to the mess. Point to the urine or feces and calmly tell your puppy "no potty here." Then scoop or sop up the accident with the paper towel. Take the evidence and the pup to the approved potty area. Drop the mess on the ground and tell the dog "good potty here," as if she had done the deed in the right place. If your pup sniffs at the evidence, praise her calmly. If the accident happened very recently your dog may not have to go yet, but wait with her a few minutes anyway. If she eliminates, praise her. Afterwards, go finish cleaning up the mess.

Soon the puppy will understand that there is a place where you are pleased about elimination and other places where you are not. Praising for elimination in the approved place will help your pup remember the rules.

Scheduling Basics

With a new puppy in the home, don't be surprised if your rising time is suddenly a little earlier than you've been accustomed to. Puppies have earned a reputation as very early risers. When your pup wakes you at the crack of dawn, you will have to get up and take her to her elimination spot. Be patient. When your dog is an adult, she may enjoy sleeping in as much as you do.

At the end of the chapter, you'll find a typical housetraining schedule for puppies aged 10 weeks to 6 months. (To find schedules for younger and older pups, and for adult dogs, visit this book's companion web site.) It's fine to adjust the rising times when using this schedule, but you should not adjust the intervals between feedings and potty outings unless your pup's behavior justifies a change. Your puppy can only meet your expectations in housetraining if you help her learn the rules.

The schedule for puppies is devised with the assumption that someone will be home most of the time with the pup. That would be the best scenario, of course, but is not always possible. You may be able to ease the problems of a latchkey pup by having a neighbor or friend look in on the pup at noon and take her to eliminate. A better solution might be hiring a pet sitter to drop by midday. A professional pet sitter will be knowledgeable about companion animals and can give your pup high-quality care and socialization. Some can even help train your pup in both potty manners and basic obedience. Ask your veterinarian and your dog-owning friends to recommend a good pet sitter.

If you must leave your pup alone during her early housetraining period, be sure to cover the entire floor of her corral with thick layers of overlapping newspaper. If you come home to messes in the puppy corral, just clean them up. Be patient—she's still a baby.

As your dog grows up, she will develop better control. But don't expect a little puppy to be able to control herself for as long as an adult can.

Use this schedule (and the ones on the companion web site) as a basic plan to help prevent housetraining accidents. Meanwhile, use your own powers of observation to discover how to best modify the basic schedule to fit your dog's unique needs. Each dog is an individual and will have her own rhythms, and each dog is reliable at a different age.

Schedule for Pups 10 Weeks to 6 Months

7:00 a.m.	Get up and take the puppy from her sleeping crate to her potty spot.
7:15	Clean up last night's messes, if any.
7:30	Food and fresh water.
7:45	Pick up the food bowl. Take the pup to her potty spot; wait and praise.
8:00	The pup plays around your feet while you have your breakfast.
9:00	Potty break (younger pups may not be able to wait this long).
9:15	Play and obedience practice.

continues

Schedule for Pups 10 Weeks to 6 Months *(continued)*

10:00	Potty break.
10:15	The puppy is in her corral with safe toys to chew and play with.
11:30	Potty break (younger pups may not be able to wait this long).
11:45	Food and fresh water.
12:00 p.m.	Pick up the food bowl and take the pup to her potty spot.
12:15	The puppy is in her corral with safe toys to chew and play with.
1:00	Potty break (younger pups may not be able to wait this long).
1:15	Put the pup on a leash and take her around the house with you.
3:30	Potty break (younger pups may not be able to wait this long).
3:45	Put the pup in her corral with safe toys and chews for solitary play and/or a nap.
4:45	Potty break.
5:00	Food and fresh water.
5:15	Potty break.
5:30	The pup may play nearby (either leashed or in her corral) while you prepare your evening meal.
7:00	Potty break.
7:15	Leashed or closely watched, the pup may play and socialize with family and visitors.
9:15	Potty break (younger pups may not be able to wait this long).
10:45	Last chance to potty.
11:00	Put the pup to bed in her crate for the night.

Appendix

Learning More About Your Jack Russell Terrier

Some Good Books

You may have to shop around for some of these books, but the hard-to-find ones are available at the web site of the Jack Russell Terrier Club of America.

Jack Russell Terriers

Atter, Sheila, *Jack Russell Terriers Today,* Howell Book House, 1995.

Britt-Hay, Deborah, *Jack Russell Terriers for Dummies*, John Wiley & Sons, 2000.

Brown, Catherine Romaine, *The Jack Russell Terrier: Courageous Companion,* Howell Book House, 1998.

James, Kenneth, *Working Jack Russell Terriers: A Hunter's Story,* Hunter House Press, 1995.

Plummer, Brian D., *The Complete Jack Russell Terrier,* Howell Book House, 1993.

Strom, Mary, *Ultimate Jack Russell Terrier*, Howell Book House, 1999.

Working Terriers

Bristow-Noble, J. C., *Working Terriers: Their Management, Training and Work,* Read Country Books, 2004.

Frain, Sean, *The Traditional Working Terrier,* Swan Hill Press, 2002.

Frier-Murza, Jo Ann, *Earthdog Ins and Outs: Guiding Natural Instincts for Success in Earthdog Tests and Den Trials*, OTR Publications, 1998.

Massey, Marilyn, *Above and Below Ground,* Woodluck Publications, 1985.

O'Conor, Pierce, *Terriers for Sport: Terrier Earth Dogs,* Read Country Books, 2005.

Care and Health

Bamberger, Michelle, DVM, *Help! The Quick Guide to First Aid for Your Dog,* Howell Book House, 1995.

DeBitetto, James, DVM, and Sarah Hodgson, *You and Your Puppy,* Howell Book House, 2000.

Giffin, James M., and Liisa D. Carlson, *Dog Owner's Home Veterinary Handbook,* 3rd edition, Howell Book House, 1999.

Messonnier, Shawn, DVM, *Natural Health Bible for Dogs and Cats: Your A–Z Guide to Over 200 Conditions, Herbs, Vitamins, and Supplements,* Three Rivers Press, 2001.

Training

Benjamin, Carol Lea, *Surviving Your Dog's Adolescence,* Howell Book House, 1993.

Benjamin, Carol Lea, *Mother Knows Best: The Natural Way to Train Your Dog,* Howell Book House, 1985.

Morn, September, *Housetraining: An Owner's Guide to a Happy Healthy Pet,* 2nd edition, Howell Book House, 2005.

Volhard, Jack, and Melissa Bartlett, *What All Good Dogs Should Know: The Sensible Way to Train,* Howell Book House, 1991.

Magazines

DogWorld
P.O. Box 37186
Boone, IA 50037-0186
(800) 896-4939
www.dogworldmag.com

True Grit
Jack Russell Terrier Club of America
P.O. Box 4527
Lutherville, MD 21094-4527
(410) 561-3655
www.terrier.com

Clubs and Registries

Jack Russell Terrier Club of America
P.O. Box 4527
Lutherville, MD 21094-4527
(410) 561-3655
www.terrier.com
This national breed club maintains an independent registry that is the largest registry of Jack Russell Terriers in the world. The club web site has information on all aspects of the breed, a list of local club representatives, breeder and rescue contact referrals, activities for pet owners and fun days, along with sanctioned trials. Don't leave without checking out the many photos of Jack Russell Terriers in the picture gallery!

American Working Terrier Association
www.dirt-dog.com/awta/index.cfm
The main objective of the AWTA is to encourage terrier and Dachshund owners to hunt with their dogs. The organization sponsors instinct and hunting tests, and publishes the *Down to Earth* newsletter.

Parson Russell Terrier Association of America
PO Box 199
North Hatfield, MA 01066
www.prtaa.org
This is the national breed club of the AKC-recognized Parson Russell Terrier. The PRTAA hosts specialty shows, fun matches, earthdog trials, and informational gatherings. The web site has information on the AKC standard, breeder and rescue contact referrals, and health issues.

The Jack Russell Terrier Club of Canada
www.jrtcc.com
Founded in 1989, the Jack Russell Terrier Club of Canada is an affiliate of the Jack Russell Terrier Club of Great Britain. This national breed club maintains an independent registry. The web site includes information about rescue groups and JRT trials in Canada.

American Kennel Club
260 Madison Avenue
New York, NY 10016
(212) 696-8200
www.akc.org
The Jack Russell Terrier was officially recognized by the AKC in 1997. In 2003 the name was changed to Parson Russell Terrier.

United Kennel Club
100 E. Kilgore Road
Kalamazoo, MI 49001-5598
(616) 343-9020
www.ukcdogs.com
The Jack Russell Terrier was recognized by the United Kennel Club in 1991.

Web Sites

American Veterinary Medical Association
www.avma.org
This web site contains the latest veterinary medical news and practical health advice for all dog owners.

Dirt-Dog.Com-Links
www.dirt-dog.com
Visit this focused and comprehensive site for a wealth of Jack Russell Terrier news, including hunting stories, results of lure coursing events, health and medical updates, JRT rescue efforts, breed club bulletins, and lots of links.

JRT Central
www.jack-russell.com
The web site of Jasper Publications, publishers of *The Jack Russell Catalog,* includes rescue stories with happy endings, favorite photographs, book recommendations, and products to purchase such as calendars and postcards. They can also be reached at P.O. Box 725, Rhinebeck, NY 12572, (845) 876-2643.

Russell Rescue Inc.
www.russellrescue.com
Russell Rescue is a rescue group of volunteers who place healthy Jack Russells of sound temperament in permanent homes. There is a network available for adoptable pets. They can also be contacted through the Jack Russell Terrier Club of America.

Index

Photo Credits:

Bonnie Nance: 1, 4–5, 8–9, 11, 12, 14, 23, 27, 28, 33, 34, 35, 37, 39, 40–41, 42, 44, 46, 55, 58, 64, 65, 67, 68, 74, 75, 76, 89, 98–99, 120, 122, 126, 128, 129, 131

Scott Whittington: 17, 83, 96

Peter Hraber: 18

Jodi Batzer: 19

Yvonne Downey: 20

Betty Dettwiler: 22

Catherine Brown: 25, 54, 91

Kent Dannen: 31

Jean M. Fogle: 47, 51, 53, 59, 61, 63, 73, 84, 125

Laurie Mercer: 80

Kathy and Walt Hawley: 81, 100

Mary Abbott/Courtesy JRTCA: 88

Courtesy JRTCA: 90

Jack Batzer: 94